学ぶ人は、変えてゆく人だ。

目の前にある問題はもちろん、

人生の問いや、

社会の課題を自ら見つけ、

挑み続けるために、人は学ぶ。

「学び」で、

少しずつ世界は変えてゆける。

いつでも、どこでも、誰でも、

学ぶことができる世の中へ。

旺文社

JN047415

受験生の
50％以下しか解けない

差がつく
入試問題 英語

三訂版

旺文社

CONTENTS

❀❀❀ スタッフ

編集協力／有限会社編集室ビーライン
校正／本多美佐保，久島智津子，山本知子
本文・カバーデザイン／伊藤幸恵 ● 本文イラスト／佐藤修一
巻頭イラスト／栗生ゑゐこ

本書の効果的な使い方

本書は，各都道府県の教育委員会が発表している公立高校入試の設問別正答率（一部得点率）データをもとに，受験生の50%以下が正解した問題を集めた画期的な一冊。解けると差がつく問題ばかりだからしっかりとマスターしておこう。

 STEP 1　出題傾向を知る

まずは，最近の入試出題傾向を分析した記事を読んで「正答率50%以下の差がつく問題」とはどんな問題か，またその対策をチェックしよう。

 STEP 2　例題で要点を確認する

出題傾向をもとに，例題と入試に必要な重要事項や，答えを導くための実践的なアドバイスを掲載。得点につながるポイントをおさえよう。

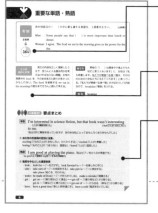

正答率が表示されています（一部オリジナル予想問題を除きます／都道府県によっては抽出データを含みます）。

多くの受験生が解けなかった原因を分析し，その対策をのせています。

入試によく出る項目の要点を解説しています。

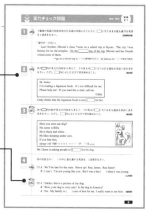

 STEP 3　問題を解いて鍛える

「実力チェック問題」には入試によく出る，正答率が50%以下の問題を厳選。不安なところがあれば，別冊の解説や要点まとめを見直して，しっかりマスターしよう。

設問ごとにチェックボックスがついています。

差がつく!!　22%　多くの受験生が解けなかった，正答率25%以下の問題には，「差がつく!!」のマークがついています。

本書がマスターできたら…　正答率50%以上の問題もしっかりおさえよう！

『受験生の50%以上が解ける　落とせない入試問題 ● 英語 [三訂版]』
本冊 96頁・別冊 24頁　定価 990円（本体900円＋税10%）

公立高校入試　徹底分析！
これが合格へのカギ！

ここでは，皆さんが受験する公立高校入試で出題される問題の内容について，
どのような傾向や特徴があるかを見ていきましょう。
出題の傾向や特徴をふまえた学習をすることによって，
これからの受験勉強の効率がアップすること間違いなし!!

● **正答率50%以下**の入試問題とは？　〜「50%以上」と比較して見てみよう〜

下の表は，「受験生の50%以上が解ける　落とせない入試問題 英語 三訂版」と「受験生の50%以下しか解けない　差がつく入試問題 英語 三訂版（本書）」に掲載されている項目の比較表です。
まずは，これらの項目を比較して，正答率が50%以下になる問題の特徴を探っていきましょう。

「受験生の50%以上が解ける　落とせない入試問題　英語　三訂版」と「受験生の50%以下しか解けない　差がつく入試問題　英語　三訂版（本書）」の掲載項目の比較表		↑ 50%以上	↓ 50%以下
文法	重要な単語・熟語	●	●
	be動詞・一般動詞	●	●
	名詞・代名詞	●	
	形容詞・副詞	●	
	前置詞	●	
	疑問文	●	
	助動詞	●	
	進行形	●	
	現在完了	●	●
	比較	●	●
	不定詞	●	●
	動名詞	●	●
	受動態	●	●
	分詞	●	●
	関係代名詞	●	●

> 「比較」や「現在完了」，品詞に関係する問題の対策は万全にしておこう！

分類	項目	⬆ 50%以上	⬇ 50%以下
文法	文のつくり（SVOO・SVOC・原形不定詞）	●	
文法	〈that＋主語＋動詞〉を含む文	●	
文法	間接疑問・疑問詞＋to *do*		●
文法	仮定法	●	●
文法	会話表現	●	
長文読解	対話の流れに合う英文を選ぶ問題	●	
長文読解	グラフのある問題	●	
長文読解	イラストのある問題	●	
長文読解	表のある問題	●	
長文読解	英文の質問に英語で答える問題	●	●
長文読解	本文の内容と合うものを選ぶ問題	●	●
長文読解	本文の内容に合うように英文を完成させる問題	●	
長文読解	テーマ・主題を選ぶ問題	●	
長文読解	下線部の内容を答える問題	●	●
長文読解	指示語の内容を答える問題	●	●
長文読解	本文の内容について日本語で答える問題	●	●
長文読解	文や語の並べ替え問題	●	●
長文読解	適切な語句を選ぶ問題	●	●
長文読解	適切な文を選ぶ問題		●
長文読解	適切な語を書く問題		●
長文読解	絵や数字を読みとる問題		●
長文読解	要約文を完成させる問題		●
英作文	日本語を英文にする問題		●
英作文	長文中の空らんを埋める英作文		●
英作文	自由英作文（絵・資料を使った問題）		●
英作文	自由英作文（手紙文を書く）		●
英作文	自由英作文（自己紹介・説明）		●

長文読解ではいろいろなパターンで出題されているぞ！

英作文の力もしっかりつけておこう！

どの分野からも出題されている。 ニガテな分野は必ず克服しておこう！

高校入試での出題分野は「読解」「英作文」「文法」「話し方・聞き方」に大きく分けられる。右のグラフを見ると、これらのどの分野からも出題されていることがわかる。なかでも「読解」の出題が一番多く、53％となっている。しかし、これは入試を突破するには「読解」の対策だけをすればよい、ということではない。「読解」問題を解くには、英文を読む力の基礎となる語いや文法の知識がなくてはならないし、英作文の力を試される設問も含まれていることが多いからである。つまり、ニガテな分野を作らず、どの分野もしっかり学習しておくことが大切なのである。また、「話し方・聞き方」（ほとんどがリスニング）は全都道府県で出題されているので、しっかり対策しよう。

〈分野別　出題数の割合〉

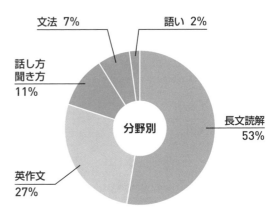

※データは、2022年に実施された全国の公立入試問題について、旺文社が独自に調べたものです。

各分野でどのような問題が出ているか、 傾向とその対策を押さえておこう！

「単語・熟語」● 「語い」問題は、単独での出題の割合は少ないが、日本語を英語にする問題や、単語の定義や意味を類推させる問題などが中心に出題されている。中学校で習った単語や熟語で定着していないものは、入試までにしっかり覚えるとともに、問題を解いていて出会った新しい単語も確実に覚えて、語い力を伸ばしていこう。

「文法」● 正しい文法知識が身についているかを「適切な語句を選ぶ問題」や「語形を変化させる問題」、「語を並べ替える問題」といった設問形式で試される。中学校で習った文法の単元をもう一度復習し、基礎をしっかり固めておこう。ニガテな単元があれば、入試までに必ず克服しておくこと。

「英作文」● 日本語を英文にする問題や自由英作文、長文中の空らんを埋める英作文など、いろいろな形式で出題されている。英作文の力の基礎となる語いや文法の知識を充実させ、日ごろから日本語を英文にしたり、身近なテーマについて英語で自分の意見を書く練習をしておこう。

「長文読解」● 対話文、物語文、エッセイなどいろいろなジャンルから、英文の質問に答える問題、内容と合う（合わない）ものを選ぶ問題、下線部の内容を答える問題などさまざまな設問形式で出題されている。解答形式は記号選択、日本語での記述、英語での記述などがある。

この分野で試されるのは，長文を読んで内容を正しく把握する読解力である。入試までにはば広いジャンルの読解問題をたくさん解いて長文を読む力を養い，本文の内容について日本語や英語で答える練習をしておくとよい。

↘「英作文」手紙文を書く問題の出題例　本文：92ページ　正答率：35%

次は，カナダに住む友達のエレン（Ellen）から送られてきた電子メールの最後の部分です。あなたなら，エレンへどのような返事を書きますか。A には 4 語以上，B には 5 語以上の英語で書きなさい。　　　　　　　　　　　　　　　　　　　　　　　　　　　〈福島県〉

エレンからの電子メール	エレンへの電子メール
This year, I'm going to study Japanese to visit you in Japan. What are you going to do this year? I hope to hear from you soon. Ellen	Hi, Ellen. Wishing you all the best in 2022. Thank you for your e-mail. I'm sending this to answer your question. I'm going to A because B .

「分詞」の問題が解けたら，差がつけられる！

「分詞」の問題はさまざまな都道府県で出題されているが，正答率は低く，難しい単元と言われている。つまり，入試までに「分詞」をマスターしておけば，ライバルに差をつけることが可能な単元ということである。現在分詞と過去分詞の違いや，文中での分詞の位置など，基礎事項を復習しなおして，自分の得意分野にしてしまおう。

↘「分詞」の出題例　本文：17ページ　正答率：21%

次の英文を最も適切な表現にするには，（　　）内のどれを用いたらよいか，記号で答えなさい。　　　　　　　　　　　　　　　　　　　　　　　　　　　　　　　　　　　〈栃木県〉

This is a temple（ア　was built　イ　has built　ウ　building　エ　built）about four hundred years ago.

- -

↘「分詞」の出題例　本文：17ページ　正答率：17%

次の対話が完成するように，（　　）内の語をすべて用いて，正しい順序に並べかえなさい。　　　　　　　　　　　　　　　　　　　　　　　　　　　　　　　　　　　　〈青森県〉

A : Are（for / books / they / children / written）?
B : Yes, they are.

重要な単語・熟語

例 題

正答率

36%

次の対話文の（　　）の中に最も適する英語を，１語書きなさい。　　〈山形県〉

Man : Some people say that (　　) is more important than lunch or dinner.

Woman : I agree. The food we eat in the morning gives us the power for the day.

ミスの傾向と対策　　英文の内容を正しく理解したうえで，空らんに入る語は何かを考えなければならない問題。女性の発言中の food を，そのまま答えた誤りが多かったかもしれない。The food を修飾する we eat in the morning の部分まできちんと読んで考える。

解き方　　男性の「（　　）は昼食や夕食よりも大切だと言う人もいます」に，女性は「私も同意します。私たちが朝食べる食べ物は，その日のための力を私たちに与えてくれます」と言っている。「私たちが朝食べる食べ物」が大切だという内容なので，breakfast「朝食」を入れる。

解 答　　breakfast

 入試必出! **要点まとめ**

単語 **I'm interested in science fiction, but that book wasn't interesting**
　　　　「(人が) 興味を持った」　　　　　　　　　　　　　　　　　　　　「(ものごとが) おもしろい」
to me.
「私はSFに興味を持っていますが，あの本は私にとっておもしろくありませんでした」

● 似た形の形容詞の区別に注意。
exciting「(ものごとが) おもしろい，わくわくする」／excited「(人が) 興奮した」
boring「(ものごとが) つまらない，退屈な」／bored「(人が) 退屈した」

熟語 **I am good at playing the piano.** 「私はピアノをひくのが得意です」
　　　be good at ＋動詞の ing 形「～するのが得意だ」

● 動詞を中心とした重要表現
・look ： look for ～「～をさがす」，look forward to ～「～を楽しみに待つ」
・take ： take care of ～「～の世話をする」，take part in ～「～に参加する」，
　　　　　take place「起こる，行われる」
・make ： be made of〔from〕～「～で作られている」，make a mistake「間違える」
・get ： get on ～「(乗り物など) に乗る」 ←→ get off ～「(乗り物など) から降りる」，
　　　　　get in ～「(車など) に乗り込む」 ←→ get out of ～「～から出る，(車など) から降りる」
・have ： have a good time「楽しい時を過ごす」，have a cold「風邪を引いている」

8

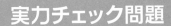

1 49%

下線部の英語の内容が次の日本語の内容に合うように，□□□に当てはまる最も適当な英語を1語書きなさい。〈愛媛県改題〉

「旅行の二日目に」

Last October, Hiromi's class *went on a school trip to Kyoto. The city *was famous for its old temples. On the [　　　] day of the trip, Hiromi and her friends visited some of them.

* go on a school trip to ～（～に修学旅行に行く）　be famous for ～（～で有名である）

2 43%

次の□内の英文の内容から考えて，下の英文の□□に当てはまる適切な英語1語を書きなさい。ただし，□内に示した文字で書き始めること。〈高知県〉

> Hi, Junko.
> I'm reading a Japanese book. It's too difficult for me.
> Please help me! If you read this e-mail, call me.
> 　　　　　　　　　　　　　　　　　　　　　Cathy

Cathy thinks that the Japanese book is not [e　　　] for her.

3 差がつく!! 25%

次の□内の絵や英文の内容から考えて，下の英文の□□に当てはまる適切な英語1語を書きなさい。ただし，□内に示した文字で書き始めること。〈高知県〉

> Have you seen our dog?
> His name is Billy.
> He is black and white.
> He likes sleeping under cars.
> If you find him,
> please call :090-××××-×××× (David Green)

Mr. Green is asking people to [1　　　] for his dog.

4

次の対話文の（　　）の中に最も適する英語を，1語書きなさい。

〔1〕 49%
A : We'll be late for the train. Hurry up! Run, James. Run faster!
B : I can't. I'm not young like you. But I was a fast (　　) when I was young.
〈山形県〉

〔2〕 差がつく!! 22%
A : Yukiko, this is a picture of my dog.
B : Wow, your dog is very cute! Is the dog in America?
A : Yes. My family is (　　) care of him for me. I really want to see him.　〈鳥取県〉

一般動詞（現在形・過去形）

正答率

↓

34%

例題

次の（　　）の中の語を最も適当な形に書きかえなさい。ただし，1語で書きかえること。　〈千葉県〉

A : This computer doesn't work.
B : Oh, really? It (break) again!

ミスの 傾向と対策

　文の時制をつかんで動詞を正しい形にする問題。Aの doesn't work（現在形）につられて breaks（3人称単数現在形）にしたり，break の過去形が書けなかったりといったミスが考えられる。文の意味を正しくとらえることが大切。また，主な動詞の過去形は確実に書けるようにしておきたい。

解き方

　Aの発言から It は this computer を指す。A「このコンピュータは動きません」 B「えっ，本当？　また壊れてしまった！」というやりとりになるので，break を過去形 broke にする。

解答　broke

　**要点まとめ**

He usually **goes** to school by bike, but he **walked** this morning.
↓
3人称単数→go に es をつける　　　　　　　　　　　過去形←過去を表す
「彼はいつもは自転車で学校に行きますが，今朝は歩いて行きました」

● **現在形は，主語が3人称単数の場合に注意！**
○主語が3人称単数→動詞の語尾に (e)s がつく。
　usually，often などの副詞が主語と動詞の間に置かれるときも (e)s をつけ忘れないように注意しよう！

● **時を表す語句を手がかりに，動詞の形を決める！**
○過去形は確実に書けるようにする。不規則動詞は特に注意！
　・規則動詞→原形に (e)d がつく。（例 play→played）
　・不規則動詞→語によって形が違う。
　　（例 buy→bought，make→made，come→came，eat→ate，go→went，send→sent，
　　leave→left，have→had）
○時を表す語句を手がかりに動詞の形を決定しよう。
　My brother (visit) Korea last summer.
　　　↓　　　　　　「この前の夏」→過去を表す
　　visited（×visit，visits，will visit）

1 (45%) 次の英文の内容から考えて，□に入る英語として最も適当なものを，下の〔　〕内の語から選び，正しい形に直して書きなさい。　〈北海道〉

〈前略〉

　　When I was making *washi*, I remembered our English teacher, Mr. Green. He came to our school from Canada last year. He said he is interested in *traditional Japanese culture. So, I decided to send one of the *washi* *postcards to him. That evening, I □ a message to him in English on it, and the next morning I sent it to him.

　　　　　　〔happen　use　stop　write　worry〕

　　　　　　　　　　　　　* traditional（伝統的な）　postcard(s)（はがき）

2 (44%) 次の（　）の中の語を最も適当な形に書きかえなさい。ただし，1語で書きかえること。　〈千葉県〉

A : Who (teach) you English last year?
B : Mr. White did.

3 (39%) 次のように尋ねられたとき，あなたはどのように答えるか，主語と動詞を含む英文を1文で書きなさい。　〈北海道〉

What time did you go to bed last night?

4 (33%) 次は，Emi と Mr. Clark の会話です。自然な会話になるように，（　）に4語以上の適切な英語を書きなさい。　〈埼玉県〉

Emi　　　　: I wrote a letter to my friend in America yesterday.
Mr. Clark : Oh, really?　(　　) about in your letter?
Emi　　　　: I wrote about my dream.
Mr. Clark : That's great.

5 (20%) 次の日本語の内容を表す英文を書きなさい。　〈山梨県〉

「私は彼に，私の学校生活について英語で話をしました。」

 現在完了

例題

正答率
↓
差がつく!!
17%

（　　）内の語を正しく並べ替えて，英文を完成させなさい。　　〈広島県〉

〈前略〉"I (visit / have / to / wanted / bridge / this / always)," Shogo said.
"I'm glad to hear that," David said.

ミスの
傾向と対策

まず this bridge をまとめ，続いて語群のhaveに着目して文を組み立てていく。have to visit this bridge や wanted to have this bridge としてしまうと，語句が余って文が成立しないので注意が必要。この have は現在完了をつくる have で，wanted は過去分詞であると気づこう。また，頻度を表す副詞 always の位置にも注意。have と過去分詞の間に置く。「私はずっとこの橋を訪れたいと思っていました」

解答　have always wanted to visit this bridge

 入試必出! **要点まとめ**

We **have lived** in this city **for** three years.
　　　　現在完了　　　　　　　「〜の間」
「私たちは3年間この市に住んでいます」

● **現在完了〈have〔has〕＋過去分詞〉の意味を確認しておこう。**
① 「〜したところだ」（完了）
We have just eaten lunch. 「私たちはちょうど昼食を食べたところです」
＊よく用いられる語→already「すでに」，yet「（疑問文で）もう，（否定文で）まだ」など
② 「〜したことがある」（経験）
I have been to Korea three times. 「私は韓国に3回行ったことがあります」
＊よく用いられる語→ever「（疑問文で）今までに」，never「一度も〜ない」など
③ 「ずっと〜している」（状態の継続）
Kate has been interested in Japan since she was a child.
　　　　　　　　　　「ケイトは子どものときからずっと日本に興味を持っています」
＊よく用いられる語→since 〜「〜以来，〜から」，for 〜「〜の間」など

● **〈動作の継続〉は現在完了進行形で表す。**
　　　　　beの過去分詞
He has been cleaning his room since he came home. 「彼は帰宅してからずっと部屋をそうじし
　　　　　　↑　　　　　　　　　　　　　　　　　　　　　　　　ています」
　　　　動詞のing形

● **現在完了は過去を表す語句といっしょに使うことはできない。**
（例）（×）He has finished his homework last night.
　　　（○）finished　　　　　　　　　　　過去を表す語句

1 次の〔1〕〜〔3〕のそれぞれの英文の（　　）の中の語を最も適当な形に書きかえて対話文として完成させなさい。ただし，1語で書きかえること。

49% 〔1〕 *A* : Do you know this song?
　　　B : Yes, I have (hear) it before, but I don't know who sings it. 〈千葉県〉

47% 〔2〕 *A* : Paul, you should start your homework after dinner.
　　　B : I've already (do) it, Mom. 〈千葉県〉

〔3〕 *A* : How long has she been (play) the piano?
　　　B : For two hours. 〈予想問題〉

2 29% 次の（　　）内から最も適当な語を1つ選び，その記号を書きなさい。 〈山梨県改題〉

　　Hello, everyone. I came to Japan three weeks ago. I have found many interesting things (ア for　イ since　ウ when　エ if) then.

3 意味の通る英文になるように，（　　）内の語句を並べ替えて，英文を完成しなさい。

36% 〔1〕 *A* : Do you play the piano?
　　　B : Yes, I do. But I (not / a / chance / had / have) to play it since I came to Japan.
　　　A : Really? Then, you can come to my house to play it.
　　　B : That's very kind of you. 〈岐阜県〉

差がつく!! 20% 〔2〕 There are some popular Japanese stories written in English here. But we (them / the children / read / have / to / never). 〈埼玉県〉

〔3〕 We (been / have / him / waiting / since / for) this morning. But he is not here yet. 〈予想問題〉

4 42% 次の対話文において，（　　）内に示されていることを伝える場合，どのように言えばよいか。　　　　　の中に，適切な英語を補いなさい。 〈静岡県〉

Yuri : Hey, John! A new student will come to our school from Tokyo!
John : Oh, really?　　　　　　　　（それは初耳だよ。）

不定詞

例題

次の対話文が完成するように，（　　）内の５つの語の中から３つを選んで正しい順番に並べかえ，その順に記号を書きなさい。（２つ不要な語があるので，それらの語は使用しないこと。）　　　　　　　　　　　　　　　〈神奈川県〉

正答率

42%

A : Where are you going to go during the summer vacation?
B : I'll go to Kyoto with my brother. He and I (ア　to　　イ　saw　ウ　see　エ　goes　オ　like) old Japanese buildings there.

ミスの傾向と対策　　与えられた語の中の動詞がsaw, see, goes, like と４つもあるので，どれを使うかを見極めるのが難しい。並べかえ問題で動詞が複数あって迷うとき，もし to も与えられていたら，不定詞〈to＋動詞の原形〉を使うことはできないか考えてみるとよい。

解き方　　主語が He and I と複数なので，続けられる動詞は saw, see, like。このうち like は〈like to＋動詞の原形〉で「～するのが好きだ」という意味を表せるので，like to see とつなげればよい。

解答　　オ→ア→ウ

 入試必出! **要点まとめ**

I have a lot of homework **to do** today.

形容詞的用法の不定詞

「私は今日するべきたくさんの宿題があります」

● **不定詞の３つの用法を確認しておこう。**
○名詞的用法「～すること」→文の主語や目的語・補語になる。
○形容詞的用法「～するべき，～するための」→直前の（代）名詞を修飾する。
○副詞的用法「～するために」（目的），「～して」（感情の原因）など→動詞や形容詞などを説明する。

● **不定詞を用いた，注意すべき構文**
○want ～ to＋動詞の原形「～に…してもらいたい」
　→want to＋動詞の原形「～したい」との違いがねらわれやすい。
　{ I want to go there. （私はそこへ行きたいです）
　{ I want you to go there. （私はあなたにそこへ行ってもらいたいです）
○tell〔ask〕～ to＋動詞の原形「～に…するように言う〔頼む〕」
○It … (for ―) to＋動詞の原形「（―にとって）～することは…だ」
○too ～ (for ―) to＋動詞の原形「あまりに～なので（―は）…できない」

● **「人やものに…させる」と言うときは，原形不定詞を使う。**
　My mother made me wash the dishes.　　　　　　　　　「母は私に皿を洗わせました」

この動詞の原形を〈原形不定詞〉という

○〈主語＋動詞＋目的語＋原形不定詞〉の形で使われる。
○あとに原形不定詞をとる動詞：
　make「～に…させる」，help「～が…するのを手伝う」，let「～に…させてやる」　など

1

（　）内の語を意味が通るように並べ替えて，**ア〜エ**の記号で答えなさい。

48%　〔1〕 Sophie（ ア　go　　イ　decided　　ウ　abroad　　エ　to ）.　　　〈栃木県〉

〔2〕（ ア　me　　イ　your　　ウ　know　　エ　let ）idea, please.　　　〈予想問題〉

2

41%　次の英文が意味の通る英文になるように，（　）内の語を並べかえて書きなさい。ただし，文頭にくる語は大文字で始めなさい。　　　〈長野県改題〉

（ fun / lot / to / a / it / play / was / of ）and walk around in the fields.

3

次の対話文の（　）の中の語を正しい語順に並べて書きなさい。

36%　〔1〕 *A* : Have you finished your homework yet, Mike?
　　　　　B : No, I haven't, Mom.
　　　　　A : I（ to / it / you / finish / told ）before dinner!　　　〈秋田県〉

32%　〔2〕〈前略〉
　　　　　Amy　　 : Well, I think（ museums / it / fun / visit / be / to / will ）. And Adelaide
　　　　　　　　　　 is called "the City of Festivals."
　　　　　Toshiko : Really? I like festivals very much.　　　〈岡山県改題〉

26%　〔3〕 *Ken*　 : Mike,（ have / you / to / do / anything ）eat?
　　　　　Mike : Yes. I have *Osenbei*. I'll give it to you.
　　　　　Ken　 : Thank you.　　　〈高知県〉

4

次の対話文の（　）内の５つの語の中から３つを選んで正しい順番に並べ替え，その順に記号を書きなさい。

差がつく!!
20%　〔1〕 *A* : Don't you think this movie is very exciting?
　　　　　B : Yes. It is very exciting. I want（ ア　be　　イ　everyone　　ウ　see
　　　　　　　　　エ　to　　オ　seen ）it.　　　〈神奈川県〉

〔2〕 *A* : Look, Tom is carrying many text books to the teachers' room.
　　　　 B : Oh, let's help（ ア　carry　　イ　him　　ウ　he　　エ　them
　　　　　　　 オ　carrying ）.　　　〈予想問題〉

15

分詞

例 題　次の対話文が完成するように，（　　）内の語をすべて用いて，正しい順序に並べかえなさい。　　　　　　　　　　　　　　　　〈青森県〉

正答率
↓
45%

A : Who (playing / that / baseball / boy / is) over there?
B : He is Ken.

ミスの
傾向と対策　　Who is playing baseball ～と続けてしまったといったミスが考えられる。ここまでは現在進行形の文として正しいが，残った that と boy がうまく続けられない。be動詞と動詞の ing形があったら，すぐに進行形と考えてしまわないようにしよう。また，動詞の ing形が名詞を修飾するときは，その位置にも注意が必要だ。

解き方　　まず Who is that boy? 「あの少年はだれですか」という疑問文を作る。playingは現在分詞と考え，playing baseball over thereが that boy を修飾するようにそのあとに置けば，「あそこで野球をしているあの少年はだれですか」という意味の文になる。

解 答　　is that boy playing baseball

入試必出!・**要点まとめ**

This is the book **written** by our teacher.
　　　　　　　　　過去分詞「～された」
「これは私たちの先生によって書かれた本です」

● **現在分詞と過去分詞を使い分けよう。語順にも注意！**
○現在分詞：「～している」
　Look at the ｜singing｜ bird. 「さえずっている鳥」

　Look at the bird ｜singing｜ in the tree. 「木でさえずっている鳥」

　→現在分詞は進行形 The bird is singing. の意味。

○過去分詞：「～された」
　Don't touch the ｜broken｜ glass. 「割れたガラス」

　Don't touch the glass ｜broken｜ during the night. 「夜の間に割られたガラス」

　→過去分詞は受動態 The glass was broken. の意味。

16

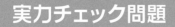

1 38%　下線部が次の意味を表すように，【　　】内の語を並べかえなさい。　〈滋賀県改題〉

『それはアメリカの女性によって書かれたすばらしい本です。』
It is【book / woman / wonderful / a / an / American / by / written】.

2 31%　次の文の意味が通るように，（　　）内の語から4語選び，それぞれ1回ずつ使って正しい語順に並べなさい。　〈福岡県改題〉

Look at the (in / wearing / is / uniforms / students) this picture.

3　意味の通る英文になるように，（　　）内の語句を正しく並べかえて書きなさい。

26%　⑴ I want to (taken / your trip / the pictures / look at / during).

〈秋田県改題〉

差がつく!! 11%　⑵ I'm in a big supermarket in *Singapore now. There are a lot of workers here. About (working / of / in / half / the people) this supermarket are over fifty years old.

*Singapore（シンガポール）

〈埼玉県〉

4 差がつく!! 21%　次の英文を最も適切な表現にするには，（　　）内のどれを用いたらよいか，記号で答えなさい。　〈栃木県〉

This is a temple (ア　was built　　イ　has built　　ウ　building　　エ　built) about four hundred years ago.

5 差がつく!! 17%　次の対話が完成するように，（　　）内の語をすべて用いて，正しい順序に並べかえなさい。　〈青森県〉

A : Are (for / books / they / children / written)?
B : Yes, they are.

関係代名詞

| 例　題 | （　　）内の語句を正しい順序に並べかえて書きなさい。　　　　　　　〈埼玉県改題〉 |

正答率
↓
39%

We (people catch / the fish / call / in) the seas near Japan *kinkai-mono*.

**ミスの
傾向と対策**　文構造を見極め，We call のあとに続く語がわかるかどうかがポイント。正答率が低かったのは，〈call＋O（目的語）＋C（補語）〉「OをCと呼ぶ」の形にすることはわかったかもしれないが，「～を」と「…と」にくる語句がそれぞれわからなかったためだと考えられる。people catch という〈主語＋動詞〉の形をどう使うかがポイント。接続詞がなくて〈主語＋動詞〉があるときは，目的格の関係代名詞が省略されているかもしれないと考えよう。

解き方　We call the fish *kinkai-mono*.「私たちはその魚を近海ものと呼ぶ」をまず組み立てる。名詞（the fish）のあとに目的格の関係代名詞が省略されて，people catch の〈主語＋動詞〉が続く形と考える。in the seas near Japan をあとに置けば完成する。

解　答　call the fish people catch in

入試必出! ● 要点まとめ

The book **(which)** you lent me was very difficult.

　　　　　目的格の関係代名詞の省略
「あなたが私に貸してくれた本はとても難しかったです」

● **関係代名詞の用法を確認しておこう。**
　関係代名詞以下の節は，前の名詞（先行詞）を修飾する。
　○先行詞が「人」…①節の主語になるとき：who〔that〕
　　　　　　　　　　②節の目的語になるとき：who〔whom, that〕
　○先行詞が「人以外」…①節の主語になるとき：which〔that〕
　　　　　　　　　　　②節の目的語になるとき：which〔that〕

先行詞の種類	主格	目的格	所有格
人	who	who〔whom〕	whose
もの・動物	which	which	whose
人・もの・動物	that	that	—

● **目的格の関係代名詞が省略された形が問われることが多い！**
　This is the bag. ＋ One of my friends gave it to me.
　　　目的格の関係代名詞が省略されている
　　　　　　　　　　↓
　→This is the bag one of my friends gave to me.
　　　名詞　　名詞の直後に〈主語＋動詞〉が続いている

1 44% 次の英文の意味が通るように，（　　）内の語から4語を選び，それぞれ1回ずつ使って正しい語順に並べなさい。　　　　　　　　　　　　　　　　　　　　〈福岡県改題〉

Here are some (are / sent / he / to / pictures) us.

2 次の英文の意味が通るように，（　　）内の語句を並べかえなさい。

差がつく!! 23% 〔1〕 No, no, don't worry about it. I have to go to the library to prepare for my speech, so I got up at six this morning. My teacher told (a lot of things / learned / speak about / I / me / to) in Japan. I'm going to speak about Japanese culture and school life in class next week. I took a lot of pictures in Japan, so I'm going to show them, too. Do you have any other good ideas about my speech?

〈長崎県B改題〉

差がつく!! 16% 〔2〕 *Paul* : Why don't you cut the sign *in the shape of an arrow?

　　　　 Yuri : Oh, Paul, that's a good idea! I will.

　　　　 Paul : By the way, can (the words / *drivers / you / read / wrote) *easily? You should make them much bigger.

　　　　 Jane : He's right. Your sign has too much information.

　　　　　　　　　　*in the shape of ～（～の形に）　driver(s)（車を運転する人）　easily（簡単に）

〈長野県改題〉

差がつく!! 14% 〔3〕 　The next morning, I went to the town library to look for some books about making *sweets and becoming a *patissier. One (I / of / found / showed / the books) that Hokkaido is famous for good sweets. There are many good shops and famous patissiers in Hokkaido, and Hokkaido *produces the best *ingredients for sweets.

　　　　　　　*sweet(s)（〈ケーキなどの〉菓子）　patissier（ケーキ職人，パティシエ）　produce（生産する）
　　　　　　　ingredient(s)（材料）

〈北海道改題〉

3 差がつく!! 22% 「私は，私に英語で話しかけてきた女性を助けました」という内容を表す英文を一つ書きなさい。　　　　　　　　　　　　　　　　　　　　　　　　　　　　　〈山梨県〉

そのほかの重要文法①（比較・動名詞・受動態）

例題

次の対話文の下線部について，（　　）内の語を並べかえ，正しい英文を完成させなさい。〈山形県〉

正答率

↓

44%

Girl : (like / which / do / sport / better / you), baseball or basketball?

Boy : Basketball.

ミスの傾向と対策　sport の位置がわからず，Which do you like sport better としてしまいがちだが，which はそれ単独で使えるほかに，〈which＋名詞〉の形で使えることも覚えておこう。Which ～ do you like better, A or B? は「AとBでは，どちらの～が好きですか」という意味。比較級 better の位置にも注意しておこう。

解き方　最後に「?」があるので疑問文の形にする。which sport で文を始め，do you like を続ける。better をこのあとに置くと，「野球とバスケットボールでは，どちらのスポーツのほうが好きですか」という意味の文になる。

解答　Which sport do you like better

 入試必出!◦ 要点まとめ

比較　Ken is <u>not</u> **as tall as** Tom.「ケンはトムほど背が高くないです」
　　　　　　　　　　　　↑
　　　　　　　　　形容詞の原級

● **比較の文の形を確認しよう。**
○He is ｜as｜ old ｜as｜ my brother.「…と同じくらい～」
　He is not ｜as｜ old ｜as｜ my brother.「…ほど～ない」
○This question is ｜more difficult｜ than that one.「…よりも～」
○Mt. Fuji is ｜the highest｜ mountain in Japan.「…の中で最も～な」

動名詞　We finished **eating** lunch.「私たちは昼食を食べ終えました」
　　　　　　　　　　動名詞（eat の ing形）

● **動名詞は文の主語，目的語，補語，前置詞の目的語になる。**
○動名詞を目的語にとる動詞：enjoy「～を楽しむ」，finish「～を終える」，stop「～をやめる」，mind「～を気にする」など
　（例文）We ｜enjoyed｜ skiing. He ｜stopped｜ walking. など
○動名詞を用いた表現
　Thank you for inviting me to the party.「～してくれてありがとう」
　How about playing soccer in the park?「～するのはどうですか」など

受動態　This house **was built** twenty years ago.「この家は20年前に建てられました」
　　　　　　　　　　　　受動態

● **受動態の形は〈be動詞＋過去分詞〉。助動詞が入る場合は〈助動詞＋be＋過去分詞〉。**
　This computer is used by many students.／The stars can be seen in the sky.

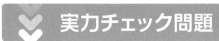

1 次の対話が完成するように，（　　）内の語をすべて用いて，正しい順序に並べかえなさい。

47% 〔1〕 *A* : Hideki does (as / run / as / not / fast) Ichiro.
　　 B : Really? 〈青森県〉

差がつく‼ 14% 〔2〕 *Shoji* : I like these two pictures. Who painted them?
　　 John : I painted this one. The (painted / was / picture / on your right) by my
　　　　　 mother.
　　 Shoji : Really? That's great. 〈高知県〉

2 （　　）内から適する語を1つ選び，その記号を書きなさい。

47% 〔1〕 Then, we used a *chemical that the small birds didn't like, but the chemical is
　　 not (ア　sell　イ　sold　ウ　buy) now. 〈奈良県改題〉
　　　　　　　　　　　　　　　　　　　　　　　　　　　　　　　　 * chemical (化学薬品)

43% 〔2〕 *A* : I couldn't sleep for a long time because I had many things to do.
　　 B : Are you all right? How about (ア　go　イ　goes　ウ　went
　　　　 エ　going) to bed early today? 〈宮崎県〉

3 次の英文の（　　）内の語を正しく並べかえ，英文を完成させなさい。

39% 〔1〕 They (in / talking / were / soft / enjoying / a) voice. 〈宮城県A改題〉

差がつく‼ 19% 〔2〕 Taking care of children is very challenging work! But I think that (important / is
　　 / spending / than / with / more / time / nothing) children. 〈埼玉県〉

差がつく‼ 22% 〔3〕 It (the / to / most / wall / difficult / was) break. 〈長野県改題〉

4 差がつく‼ 15% 次の日本語の意味を表すように，（　　）内の語を並べかえなさい。 〈滋賀県改題〉

『それは，さまざまなものを運ぶのに使われます。』
It (to / kinds / used / things / carry / many / is / of).

そのほかの重要文法②（間接疑問・疑問詞＋to *do*）

次の日本文の意味に合う英文になるように，（　　）内の語を並べ替えなさい。

〈北海道〉

正答率

↓

差がつく!!

15%

どの電車に乗るべきか教えてください。

Please tell me (I / which / should / train) take.

ミスの
傾向と対策

「どの電車に乗るべきか」が，動詞 tell の２つ目の目的語になっている文。〈疑問詞＋名詞〉の which train「どの電車」で始まる間接疑問になることに気づこう。間接疑問は疑問詞のあとが〈主語＋動詞〉の語順になる。通常の疑問文の語順と混同して which train should I take としないよう注意。間接疑問の問題では，必ずと言っていいほど〈疑問詞＋主語＋動詞〉の語順が理解できているかどうかが問われる。

解 答　which train I should

 入試必出! **要点まとめ**

〈疑問詞＋主語＋動詞〉

間接疑問 I don't know **why he is crying**.「私はなぜ彼が泣いているのかわかりません」
間接疑問

● **間接疑問の語順は〈疑問詞＋主語＋動詞〉！**
○疑問詞で始まる疑問文がほかの文に組み込まれたものを間接疑問という。
○間接疑問は，動詞の目的語になる。語順は〈疑問詞＋主語＋動詞〉となることに注意。

What did you buy?　「あなたは何を買いましたか」

Please tell me **what**　　you bought.「あなたが何を買ったか私に教えてください」
　　　　　　　疑問詞　　　主語　動詞

○間接疑問の疑問詞が主語のときの語順は〈疑問詞＋動詞〜〉の語順。

I don't know　**who**　　called me yesterday.「私は昨日だれが私に電話したのかわかりません」
　　　　　　疑問詞＝主語　　動詞

疑問詞＋to *do* Please tell me **when** to leave.「いつ出発したらよいか私に教えてください」
　　　　　　　　　　　　〈疑問詞＋to *do*〉

● **〈疑問詞＋to *do*〉は疑問詞ごとの意味を押さえる！**
○how to *do*「どう〜したらよいか，〜のしかた」
　My father taught me how to play the guitar.「父が私にギターの弾き方を教えてくれました」
○what to *do*「何を〜したらよいか〔すべきか〕」
○where to *do*「どこで〔へ〕〜したらよいか〔すべきか〕」
○when to *do*「いつ〜したらよいか〔すべきか〕」

1 (40%) 次の（　　）に当てはまる最も適当な英語を**ア**〜**エ**から選び，その記号を書きなさい。

〈山梨県〉

Your mother knew (**ア** how 　**イ** what 　**ウ** when 　**エ** where) hard you practiced volleyball.

2 次の（　　）の中の**ア**〜**オ**を，意味が通るように並べ替え，記号で答えなさい。　〈静岡県〉

(1) (32%) *A* : (**ア** is 　**イ** know 　**ウ** how much 　**エ** do you 　**オ** this *tenugui*) ?
B : Let's see ... look, it's 800 yen.

(2) (29%) You can buy cakes, *sakuramochi* and many other *sweets. Can (**ア** sweet 　**イ** which 　**ウ** decide 　**エ** to 　**オ** you) buy?

* sweet（甘い菓子）

3 次の（　　）内の語句を，意味が通る英文になるように並べ替えなさい。

(1) (37%) I can't (will / what / be / our / imagine / lives) like when we're older. 〈埼玉県〉

(2) (41%) 〔*In a park*〕
A : It is getting dark. Do you (is / what / it / time / know) now?
B : Yes. It will be six o'clock soon. 〈福島県〉

(3) (43%) Last May, I went to my grandfather's house with my friend, Carol. There, my grandfather (to us / grow / showed / how) rice. Carol, my grandfather and I went to the *rice field in the morning.

* rice field（田んぼ）

〈埼玉県〉

仮定法

| 例 題 | 次の英文を日本文にしなさい。　　　　　　　　　　　　　　　〈予想問題〉

If I lived in New York, I would go to see a musical every day. |

ミスの傾向と対策　　If I に続く動詞が過去形 lived になっていること，文の後半に助動詞 will の過去形 would があることから，仮定法の文だとわかる。仮定法は，現実とは異なることや，実現する可能性がほとんどない願望を表す。日本文にする問題では，動詞の時制に注意し，仮定法の文かどうかを見極めよう。仮定法には，if ～を用いた「もし～なら，…のになあ」や，I wish ～「～ならいいのになあ」などの表現がある。

解 答　もし私がニューヨークに住んでいたら，毎日ミュージカルを見に行くでしょう〔見に行くのになあ〕。

 入試必出!・要点まとめ

If ～ **If Yumi had a passport, she could travel abroad.**
　　　　動詞の過去形　　　　　　　　助動詞の過去形
「もしユミがパスポートを持っていれば，海外旅行に行けるのに」
※実際は，パスポートを持っていないので，海外旅行に行けない。

I wish ～ **I wish I had a sister.**「私に姉〔妹〕がいればなあ」　※実際は，姉〔妹〕がいない。
　　　　　(助)動詞の過去形

● **現在の事実とは異なることや，実現する可能性がほとんどない願望は仮定法で表す!**
○〈If＋主語＋動詞の過去形，主語＋would〔could〕＋動詞の原形〉
　「もし～なら，…するのに〔できるのに〕」　　　　　　…現在の事実とは異なることを述べる
○〈I wish＋主語＋(助)動詞の過去形〉「～ならなあ」　…実現する可能性がほとんどない願望を述べる

● **仮定法での be動詞は，主語に関わらず were を使うことが多い。**
　If I were a good baseball player, I could join a game.
　　「もし私が上手な野球選手だったら，試合に出られるのに」
　I wish Jackson were here.
　　「ジャクソンがここにいればなあ」
　　※話し言葉では was を使うこともある。

1 次の（　）内の語句を，意味が通る英文になるように並べ替えなさい。ただし，不要な語句が1つずつあるので，それは使用しないこと。 〈予想問題〉

〔1〕 I wish (an / would / in / there / amusement park / were) my town.

〔2〕 (phone number / I / her / if / knew / know), I could call her right now.

〔3〕 (help / if / I / I / you / wish / could), but I have no time now.

2 次の対話文が成立するように，□□□に入れるのに適する内容を考えて，英語で書きなさい。 〈予想問題〉

A : Who is the boy in this picture?
B : My friend Mark. He went back to America last year.
A : I see. Do you miss him?
B : Yes. I wish ☐☐☐☐☐☐☐.

3 次の英文を日本文にしなさい。 〈予想問題〉

I wish I were better at cooking.

4 次の日本文を英文にしなさい。 〈予想問題〉

〔1〕 もし私があなたなら，その本は買わないでしょう。

〔2〕 私の家がもっと広ければなあ。

5 次の問いに対するあなた自身の答えを，5語以上の英語で書きなさい。 〈予想問題〉

If you had more free time, what would you do?

長文読解（適切な語句を選ぶ）

例題

駅で待ち合わせをしていた Mikako と Beth との次の対話で，（A）及び（B）の中にそれぞれ入る語の組み合わせとして正しいものは，次の**ア～エ**のどれですか。 〈東京都〉

正答率

↓

49%

Mikako : Oh, did you come by bike, Beth?

Beth : Yes. Where can I *park my bike, Mikako?

Mikako : Over there. Parking is *free for the first two hours.

Beth : It's ten o'clock now. So I don't need to *pay any money before (A) o'clock. Right?

Mikako : That's right. After the first two hours, you need to pay fifty yen for each hour.

Beth : I see.

Mikako : We have to buy some presents for our friends, eat lunch, and look for some books today.

Beth : Yes. I think it will take three hours, so I'll need to pay (B) yen for parking.

* park（駐輪する） free（無料の） pay（支払う）

ア （A）eleven （B）fifty **イ** （A）eleven （B）one hundred and fifty

ウ （A）twelve （B）fifty **エ** （A）twelve （B）one hundred and fifty

ミスの傾向と対策 　（A）は解法のポイントとなる 3，4 行目の for the first two hours と don't need to ～ の意味がとれなかったというミスが考えられる。(B) はそれまでの会話の流れをすべて把握していないと解けないので，難しかったのかもしれない。2 人は駐輪代について話しているので，駐輪する時間と料金に関する数字や表現をしっかり押さえながら読みすすめるようにする。

解き方 　（A）を含む文は「～時前ならお金を払う必要がない」の意味。直前のミカコの発言に「最初の 2 時間は駐輪は無料」とある。今 10 時なので，「12」時前なら無料。(B) を含む文は「3 時間かかると思うから，駐輪代に～円支払う必要があるだろう」の意味。ミカコの 3 番目の発言に「最初の 2 時間後は 1 時間ごとに 50 円支払う必要がある」とあるので，駐輪代は「50」円。

解答 ウ

 入試必出! **要点まとめ**

She looked **happy** when she got a birthday present from him.

　〈look ＋形容詞〉：「～に見える」

「彼女は彼から誕生日のプレゼントをもらってうれしそうでした」

● **空らんに入る語を推測し，前後の文脈から考えて，空らんにあてはまる語を選択しよう!**

　最初に，空らんの前後から，入る語の品詞は何かなどを推測しよう。空らんの前後を見ただけで，文法・熟語の知識で解ける場合もあるが，そうでない場合は前後の文脈から考えて，あてはまる語を選択する。解法のカギとなる文をすばやく見つけることが大切。

1 (44%) 次の英文は，有紀さんとアメリカ出身のグリーン先生 (Mr. Green) との会話です。これを読んで，あとの問いに答えなさい。　　　　　　　　　　　　　〈滋賀県改題〉

Yuki : I learned a very simple but important thing.

Mr. Green : Oh, what is it?

Yuki : In Australia the people I met always said hello to me with a smile. That made me happy. I also found that my host family often said thank you to each other. Saying hello and thank you is good for communication. Now I'd like to say these words to people around me more often.

Mr. Green : That's nice. In America my parents always told their children to say please and thank you to others. They called these words *magic words. For example, if I said, "Give me juice," my mother said, "What's the magic word?" Then, I had to say, "Juice, please," or "(　) have some juice, please?"

Yuki : My parents also told me to *greet others when I was a little girl.

Mr. Green : I love Japanese *greetings. My favorite ones are *ittekimasu* and *itterasshai*. It's nice to hear these words from people living near me. I feel these greetings make a warm *connection between people.

Yuki : I agree. I'm going to send Jane a card to say thank you. I really want to write a good message.

Mr. Green : Good. Why don't you write the things you learned in Australia? I think Jane will like it.

Yuki : Nice idea! Thank you.

＊magic（魔法の）　greet（あいさつする）　greeting(s)（あいさつ）　connection（つながり）

本文中の（　）に入る最も適当なものを，次の**ア**～**エ**から１つ選びなさい。

ア Will you　**イ** Can you　**ウ** Shall I　**エ** May I

2 次の英文は，南アメリカの先住民に伝わる，クリキンディ（Kurikindi）という名前のハチドリ（a hummingbird）の短い物語を題材に書かれたものです。（ ① ）～（ ③ ）に，最もよく当てはまる語を，それぞれ下の**ア**～**カ**から１つ選び，記号で答えなさい。

〈宮崎県改題〉

I'd like to introduce a short story of a hummingbird. A hummingbird is a very little bird. The little bird's name in this story is Kurikindi.

*Kurikindi lived in a forest. One day there was a *fire in the forest. The little bird stayed there and tried to *put out the fire. But all the other animals hurried to *escape. When they saw Kurikindi on the way, they asked Kurikindi, "Why are you doing that?" Kurikindi answered, "I'm only doing something I can do."*

☐☐☐ ①43%　After (①) this short story, I thought about a few things. For example, did the hummingbird believe he could put out the fire? Why did all the other animals want to escape from the forest?

☐☐☐ ②40%　Kurikindi did (②) so small that others thought his *actions meant (③). Many people often think like that. What do you think about Kurikindi?

☐☐☐ ③31%

* fire（火事）　put out（消す）　escape（逃げる）　action（行動）

ア read　　**イ** something　　**ウ** reading　　**エ** came
オ excuse　　**カ** nothing

---

3 次の文章を読んで，問いに答えなさい。

〈千葉県改題〉

☐☐☐ Ⓐ38%　I am a junior high school student. Last year the *Volleyball World Cup *was held in my city, and a lot of volunteers were (Ⓐ) for the *event. My sister worked to help many *foreigners as an *English speaking guide at the station.

☐☐☐ Ⓑ44%　One day, I went to the station to see my sister, but I found she was *busy. Then, a foreigner came to me and said, "(Ⓑ) bus stops at the *arena?" I answered in English, "Take ... take the No. 6 bus, please." I was able to answer without my sister's help! It was a good *experience. I've studied English harder since that day.

* Volleyball World Cup（バレーボールワールドカップ大会）　be held（開催される）　event（催し）
foreigner（外国人）　English speaking guide（英語が話せるガイド）　busy（忙しい）
arena（アリーナ・競技場）　experience（経験）

本文中の（ Ⓐ ）（ Ⓑ ）の中に入る最も適当なものを次の**ア**～**エ**のうちからそれぞれ１つずつ選び，その記号を書きなさい。

Ⓐ **ア** fallen　　**イ** helped　　**ウ** needed　　**エ** told
Ⓑ **ア** Why　　**イ** When　　**ウ** Where　　**エ** Which

4 ⟨38%⟩ 次の英文は，早紀が，卒業 (graduation) を記念して取り組んでいる活動について，英語を
教えているラッド (Ladd) 先生と会話している場面のものです。これを読んで，問いに答
えなさい。 〈北海道改題〉

Mr. Ladd : Hi, Saki. I hear you worked hard to make the *yearbook. How was it?

Saki : It was fun. I finished making it with my friends last week. There are
many pictures of school *events in it, for example, the school trip and the
sports festivals. We hope the yearbook will be a great *memento for all
*the third-year students.

Mr. Ladd : I think they'll be happy to see pictures of their school life after
graduation. How did you get pictures for the yearbook?

Saki : We (　　) our friends and teachers to bring pictures of our school events.
They gave us about three hundred pictures, but we *couldn't use all of
them. So, we *chose one hundred pictures.

Mr. Ladd : Was it difficult to choose good pictures, Saki?

Saki : Yes. But we enjoyed making the yearbook. Now we're doing another
thing for our graduation, Mr. Ladd.

Mr. Ladd : What is it?

Saki : We want to show the third-year students a video to *look back on our
school life, and we're making it now. For the music in it, I'll play the
piano.

Mr. Ladd : I think your music will make the video wonderful.

Saki : I hope so. *The day before our graduation, the third-year students will
watch it in the *gym. You can see yourself in the video.

Mr. Ladd : Really?

Saki : Yes. Do you remember you *sang with us at the school festival? You'll
watch the *scene in the video. I'll be happy if you join us on that day,
Mr. Ladd.

Mr. Ladd : Thank you. I'm glad to hear that. I think the things you're doing for
your graduation will be a good *memory for you.

Saki : Thank you.

> ＊yearbook（卒業記念アルバム） event(s)（行事） memento（思い出の品）
> the third-year student(s)（3年生） couldn't ～ all（すべてを～できたわけではなかった）
> chose（choose（選ぶ）の過去形） look back on（～を振り返る） the day before（～の前日）
> gym（体育館） sang（sing の過去形） scene（場面） memory（思い出）

本文の内容から考えて，（　　）に入る英語として最も適当なものを，次の中から選び，正
しい形に直して書きなさい。

| raise | ask | look | listen |

長文読解（適切な文を選ぶ）

次の英文は，中学生の智子（Tomoko）さんが書いた英語のスピーチ原稿の一部です。あとの問いに答えなさい。　　　　　　　　　　　　　　　　　　　〈宮崎県改題〉

正答率

↓

差がつく‼

20%

　　My grandma is 71 years old, and she always wants to try something new. She likes playing sports, listening to pop music, and so on. One day, she asked me to teach her and her friends how to use computers. I said to her, "(　　) But it's difficult for you to use computers. I'm afraid you can't do it." Then she took out a newspaper and said, "How do you know that? Many *elderly people are now using computers. Tomoko, please read this."

* elderly people（高齢者）

（　　）に入る最も適切なものを，次の**ア～エ**から1つ選び，記号で答えなさい。

ア　No way.　　**イ**　Thanks a lot.　　**ウ**　I think so too.　　**エ**　I'd love to.

ミスの傾向と対策　　この設問は，直前の文の she asked me to teach ～ の意味が取りづらく，空らんには依頼に対する返事が入ることがわかりづらい。また，選択肢の No way.「とんでもない」が紛らわしい。解法のカギとなる慣用表現なども覚えておこう。

解き方　　直前の文に「ある日，彼女（＝祖母）は私に彼女と彼女の友だちにコンピュータの使い方を教えてくれるように頼みました」とあるので，「私は彼女に『喜んで〔ええ，ぜひとも〕。でもあなた方にとってコンピュータを使うことは難しいわ。あなた方にはできないのではないかと思うわ』と言いました」となるよう，I'd love to. を選ぶ。I'd love to. は誘いや依頼，提案などを快諾するときに用いる表現。

解答　**エ**

**要点まとめ**

Would you like to go to the movies with me? — **I'd love to.**
「私と映画に行きませんか」　　　　　　　　　　　　「ええ，ぜひとも」

● **空らんの前後の文に注目しよう！**
　適切な文を選ぶ問題では前後のやりとりに注目して，入れるべき文を考えよう。そのときに，決まった受け答えのパターンや慣用表現などを覚えておくと解きやすくなる。

● **よく出る慣用表現**
　・Shall I ～?「～しましょうか」— Yes, please.「ええ，お願いします」
　・Will〔Can〕you ～?「～してくれませんか」— Sure. / All right.「いいですよ」
　・Would you like ～?「～はいかがですか」— No, thank you.「いいえ，けっこうです」

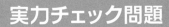 次の英文は，康平が，日本とアメリカ（America）の学校の違いについて，アメリカから来たテッド（Ted）と会話している場面のものです。これを読んで，問いに答えなさい。

〈北海道改題〉

Kohei : Hi, Ted. What are you doing?

Ted 　 : I'm writing a letter to my brother, Jim. I got a letter from him yesterday.

Kohei : What did he write in his letter?

Ted 　 : He wrote he'll *enter high school next month. He's really *looking forward to his new school life.

Kohei : Next month? Does school start in September?

Ted 　 : That's right. In my country, it usually starts in September and *ends in June. We have *more than two months for summer vacation.

Kohei : Really! That's very different. Can you tell me any other differences you've *found between your school in America and this school? I'm interested in them.

Ted 　 : OK, Kohei. For example, one of the differences is lunch in the classroom.

Kohei : ☐

Ted 　 : Well, at my school in America, students don't have lunch in their classrooms. They go to the *school cafeteria to have the lunch they bring from home. They can also buy their lunch there.

Kohei : I didn't know that.

Ted 　 : Another big difference is school uniforms. I learned about school uniforms before I came to Japan, but I'm still surprised to see that all the students at this school wear a school uniform.

Kohei : I hear *most of the schools in America don't have school uniforms.

Ted 　 : *Exactly. My school doesn't have a school uniform. So, I enjoy wearing my school uniform. It's a new *experience for me.

Kohei : I think you've learned many new things since you came here.

Ted 　 : Yes. Finding the differences is interesting to me.

Kohei : I agree. I want to talk more about school life in America.

Ted 　 : Sure, Kohei. I also have some things to ask you about school life in Japan.

Kohei : OK, Ted. The next class will start soon. Let's talk later.

Ted 　 : Nice to talk with you, Kohei.

　　　* enter（入学する）　look forward to（〜を楽しみにする）　end（終わる）　more than（〜より多い）
　　　found（find の過去分詞形）　school cafeteria（学校内の生徒用の食堂）　most of（ほとんどの〜）
　　　exactly（そのとおり）　experience（経験）

本文の内容から考えて，☐に入る英文として最も適当なものを，**ア**〜**エ**から選びなさい。

ア　When do students in Japan go to a school cafeteria?

イ　What did you have for lunch?

ウ　What do you mean?

エ　How do you like your school life here?

長文読解（適切な語を書く）

例題

Masato と ALT の Mr. Jeffrey の【学校での会話】の一部を読んで，問いに答えなさい。

〈埼玉県改題〉

正答率

↓

26%

【学校での会話】

Masato : You look so happy, Mr. Jeffrey. You're smiling.

Mr. Jeffrey : Oh, hi, Masato. I was listening to a CD. It's English *rakugo*.

Masato : *Rakugo*, a Japanese *comic story? What's the story about?

Mr. Jeffrey : It's about a man who is looking for a job. But he doesn't want to work very hard. He finds an easy job in a zoo, and *funny things happen there. I've ( ) to this story many times, and I can still *laugh. *Rakugo* shows that Japanese people have a great *sense of humor. You'll also find interesting things about Japanese culture in *rakugo*.

* comic story（こっけいな話） funny（こっけいな） laugh（笑う）
sense of humor（ユーモアのセンス）

（ ）にあてはまる最も適切な1語を，英語で書きなさい。

ミスの傾向と対策 　空らんには動詞が入ることと，どんな動詞が入るかはおおよそ推測できると思うが，正答率は低かった。動詞を正しい形で答えられなかったというミスが考えられる。動詞を入れる場合は，前後をよく見て時制を判断し，正しい形で答えよう。動詞の前にある語や時を表す副詞（句）に注目するとよい。

解き方 　I've（＝I have）のあとなので，〈have＋過去分詞〉の現在完了の文にする。「私はこの話を何度も～したことがあり，それでも笑えます」という文。「聞いた（ことがある）」とするのが適切。直後の to に注目する。「～を聞く」は listen to ～ なので，listen の過去分詞を入れる。

解答 listened

 入試必出！ 要点まとめ

I've visited Kyoto many times, so I know a lot about the city.

〈have＋過去分詞〉…現在完了

「私は何度も京都を訪れたことがあるので，その都市についてたくさん知っています」

● **動詞は文に合った形で答える。**

英文に動詞を補充するときは，前後をよく見て時制を考え，正しい形で答えるようにしよう。

・〈have〔has〕＋過去分詞〉⇒現在完了
・〈be動詞＋～ing〉⇒進行形
・〈be動詞＋過去分詞〉⇒受動態
・〈Let's＋動詞の原形～.〉⇒勧誘表現

1 38%　英語の授業で，ALT（外国語指導助手）の Mr. White が日本で興味深く感じたことを，また，ホームステイから帰国した健二（Kenji）がアメリカで興味深く感じたことを，それぞれ話しました。次の2つのスピーチを読んで，問いに答えなさい。　　　　〈山梨県改題〉

【Mr. White's Speech】

Hello, everyone. I came to Japan three weeks ago. I have found many interesting things since then. I will talk about some of them.

The first thing is about the Japanese word "*doumo*." I know that it means "thank you." But one day I said to a teacher, "Hello," and he said, "*Doumo*." I was very surprised. Later my friend taught me many meanings of "*doumo*." For example, it means "thank you," "hello," and sometimes "sorry." I think it is very useful. Small words like this are important for communication.

Second, it is easy to get things that I need. I saw many kinds of *vending machines selling drinks, rice, and sometimes eggs in Yamanashi. Also there are many convenience stores in Japan. When I bought something there, I didn't have to say many Japanese words. But I am studying Japanese now, so I want to speak Japanese more.

The last thing is a peace sign. I like taking pictures. One day after school when I tried to take pictures of my students, they made a peace sign with their fingers. Yesterday, in another class, the same thing happened. I don't know why they make a peace sign when they are in pictures.

That's all. Thank you for listening.

【Kenji's Speech】

Hi, everyone. I have just come back from America. I stayed with Mr. Baker's family for ten days during the summer vacation. I had a wonderful time. Today I am going to talk about three interesting things that I found there.

First, their English was very fast for me. So I didn't understand what they said. But people around me were very kind. They tried to speak more slowly. Sometimes they used pictures to tell me something. I think I have to study English harder to understand them.

Second, everything was very big. One day my host family took me (　　) a hamburger shop. I ordered one hamburger and one large cola. When I saw the large cola, I was very surprised. The large cola was much bigger than a large cola in Japan. It was as big as my face.

Third, I didn't know when to start and finish eating. In Japan we say, "*Itadakimasu*," before eating and, "*Gochisousama*," after eating. But in America they didn't say any special words to start and finish eating.

Thank you.

* vending machine（自動販売機）

（　　）に当てはまる最も適当な1語を，本文の内容に合うように，書きなさい。

次の英文は，よしこさんが英語の宿題で書いた日記の一部です。これを読んで，次の問い
に答えなさい。

〈滋賀県改題〉

よしこさんの日記

Today, Mr. Brown, my father's friend, visited us. He was *curious about many things in our house. A few minutes later, he was taking some pictures of *bonsai* in our *garden. I didn't see why he was doing that because it was not very interesting for me. So I tried to ask him some questions. I said, "Excuse me," and asked, "(   ) taking pictures of it?" He answered, "Because I want to send them to my friends in America. I will tell them how nice Japanese *bonsai* is." He liked its beautiful small tree and *moss.

We talked for a long time and I was surprised that he knew a lot about Japan. I think Japan has good things which I didn't notice. For example, *furoshiki* is one of them. It is used to carry many kinds of things. Maybe, some Japanese people say, "We know our country well because we live here." But that is wrong. I want to learn about Japan more through talking with foreign people.

* curious（好奇心が強い） garden（庭） moss（苔）

（   ）に適当な英語を3語入れて，よしこさんがブラウンさん（Mr. Brown）にした質問
を完成させなさい。

3 次の対話は，高校生の由実とアメリカから来た留学生のジェーンが放課後に話したものであり，由実はジェーンにメモを見せているところです。これに関してあとの問いに答えなさい。

〈広島県改題〉

Yumi : I want to talk with you about our *school trip to Tokyo and some other places. We have about five months before the trip, and you know each group has to make a *plan for the second day soon. I have an idea about our group's plan. Look at this.

Jane : Sure, so on this day our group will go to a *museum of *literature in the morning, and we will stay there for two hours. I see. Yumi, I love such a museum! This is an important place to visit because our group members are interested in writing stories.

Yumi : Good! I know Tokyo has a good museum. There are many things which *are related to Japanese *writers and we can see some of them. I've been there, and it was very good.

Jane : That's nice! This is really a good idea. I think the members can learn a lot there.

Yumi : I think so, too. But I don't know which place we will visit after lunch. We can stay at one place for three hours. Do you have any idea?

Jane : Well, how about a *university? I want to hear a *lecture about Japanese literature there.

Yumi : That's a good idea. Let's (　　) the other members about our plan tomorrow. I think they will agree.

Jane : Yes! I'll be very happy if I can visit these places. I want to learn more about Japanese literature. Teaching Japanese literature in my country is my dream.

Yumi : Really? That's a nice dream. You will become a good teacher.

Jane : Thanks. Yumi, do you have a dream?

Yumi : I want to write children's books in the *future. I hope many children in the world will read my books.

Jane : Great! I want to read your books, too.

Yumi : Thank you, Jane. Our school trip will be a good *chance to think about our future.

> * school trip（修学旅行）　plan（計画）　museum（博物館）　literature（文学）
> be related to ～（～に関係がある）　writer（作家）　university（大学）　lecture（講義）　future（将来）
> chance（機会）

本文中の（　　）に適切な語を必要なだけ補って，英文を完成させなさい。

長文読解（本文の内容に合う文を完成させる）

例題

正答率
↓
46%

次の対話の文章を読んで，あとの問いに答えなさい。　　　　　　〈東京都改題〉

Robin ： Thank you very much for your help, Yukie and Haruto. You're very good teachers for us.

Ailing ： Yeah, *thanks to your help, my new life in Tokyo is easier.

Yukie ： We're very glad to hear that.

Haruto ： You're welcome, Robin and Ailing. It's also a good chance for me to practice speaking English. *Just as English is not easy for me, I think Japanese is hard for foreign people.

Robin ： Yes. I've lived here in Tokyo for more than three years. So speaking Japanese and understanding spoken Japanese are not so difficult for me now. But reading and writing Japanese are still hard. There are three kinds of *characters in Japanese.

Haruto ： Do you mean *hiragana*, *katakana*, and *kanji*?

Robin ： <u>That's right.</u> And many *kanji* are read in two or more ways. It's very hard for me to learn how to use *kanji*.

　　　　　　　　* thanks to ~ （~のおかげで）　just as ~ （~であるように）　character（文字）

下線部の内容を，次のように書き表すとすれば，□□□ の中にどれが入りますか。

For me, reading and writing Japanese are hard because □□□.

ア　many *kanji* are read in two or more ways

イ　there are three kinds of characters in Japanese

ウ　I have lived in Tokyo for more than three years

エ　I have never learned *hiragana*, *katakana*, or *kanji*

ミスの傾向と対策　　　下線部の That が指す内容が英文のどこの部分なのかをさがすとき，迷ったかもしれない。設問の英文が，本文のどこに述べられているか，どのように言いかえられているかということをていねいにさがそう。

解き方　　Robin の2つ目の発言に reading and writing Japanese are still hard とあり，その直後で Haruto は three kinds of characters の内容を述べているので，ここが解答の部分だと予測できる。

解答　イ

　**要点まとめ**

It is very interesting to learn about foreign cultures.

It is … to ~. 「~することは…だ」　　　　　　「外国の文化について学ぶことはとてもおもしろいです」

● **内容一致文完成では言いかえ表現がよく使われる！**

　本文の表現が言いかえられていることがあるので，言いかえ表現を覚えておこう。

① There is〔are〕B in A. ⇒ A has〔have〕B. 「A には B がある」

② can ~ ⇒ be able to ~ 「~できる」

③ ~ after … 「…したあとで~」 ⇒ … before ~ 「~する前に…」

1 〔41%〕　次の英文を読んで，あとの問いに答えなさい。　〈青森県改題〉

Today I will tell you about a man I have known for about fifteen years. He was one of my students and his name is *Kenji.

When he was seventeen years old, I asked him what he wanted to do in the future. He couldn't say anything.

One day he found a *poster of a *cookery school. It said, "We'll have an *open house next Saturday. Let's enjoy cooking together!" He was interested in cooking and cooked for his family many times. So, he went there.

The students of the school *welcomed him. He had a very good time there because he cooked with them and enjoyed the food. He thought, "Cooking is a lot of fun. If I become a *cook, I can make many kinds of food. Good food can make people happy. I'll become a cook."

When he finished high school, he went to the cookery school. The classes were very difficult, but it was exciting for him to study something new every day. He studied very hard there to be a cook.

After he finished studying at the cookery school, he came to this city. He started to work for a Japanese restaurant. In his first year, he only *washed the *dishes. When he *was washing the dishes, sometimes he watched the things that the other *cooks did. This was his *way of learning how to cook Japanese food.

One day in his second year, the *master chef told him to cook lunch. Kenji was surprised. The master chef said, "I will watch how you cook. And if your lunch is good, you may help the other cooks." He watched how Kenji cooked.

He finished cooking, but the master chef didn't eat the lunch. Kenji asked him why. "You *did your best today and I think you studied hard at the cookery school, but you didn't cook in my way ... I know you feel sad, but I want all the cooks here to become good cooks. You must learn how to cook in my way first. After that, you can cook *as you like. Don't *rush. You have a lot of time."

Kenji *faced many *difficulties when he was working. Sometimes it was hard for him to *overcome them, but he never *gave up and became a good cook.

*Kenji（けんじ）　poster（ポスター）　cookery school（料理学校）　open house（体験入学）
welcomed（〜を歓迎した）　cook（料理人）　washed（〜を洗った）　dishes（食器）
was washing（〜を洗っていた）　cooks（cook（料理人）の複数形）　way（やり方）　master chef（料理長）
did your best（最善をつくした）　as you like（好きなように）　faced（〜に直面した）
difficulties（困難）　overcome（〜を克服する）　gave up（あきらめた）

本文の内容と合うように，次の英文に続けるのに最も適切なものを，ア〜エの中から一つ選びなさい。

The master chef told Kenji to cook in the master chef's way because

ア　he wanted him to know what to cook.

イ　he wanted to give his restaurant to Kenji.

ウ　he wanted him to cook well.

エ　he wanted to eat a good lunch.

2 34%　次の英文は，英語の先生（Kazuko）が，卒業する生徒へのメッセージとして文集にのせるために，ホームステイ（homestay）の体験について書いたものです。あとの問いに答えなさい。　　　　　　　　　　　　　〈宮崎県改題〉

　　When I was little, I was often sick. I was *shy too. My parents and other people did everything for me. I usually didn't have to ask them to help me. I was always waiting for someone to do everything for me. So I didn't have to *express myself.

　　When I was in elementary school, I liked music and practiced the piano every day. I went to an English *conversation school every week because I was interested in American movies and going to America.

　　　　　　　　　　　　　　　* shy（内気な）　express（表現する）　conversation（会話）

次の英文を，本文の内容と合うように完成させるのに，最も適切なものを，ア～エから1つ選び，記号で答えなさい。

When Kazuko was in elementary school, ⬚⬚⬚⬚⬚⬚⬚⬚⬚⬚.
　ア　she liked talking with her friends
　イ　she played the piano for people around her
　ウ　she often went to the movies with her sisters
　エ　she thought of visiting America

3 47%　次の英文は，Ayaka が書いた作文です。これを読んで，問いに答えなさい。　　〈埼玉県改題〉

　　Last summer twenty students from a sister city in Australia visited Japan. They went to Tokyo and then came to my city. For the last three days each student stayed with a Japanese family. Diana stayed with us. My family *welcomed her and enjoyed talking with her. Her Japanese was very good because she was learning Japanese in her school. She was interested in Japanese culture.

　　When we had dinner, Diana asked us a question about hotel room numbers in Japan. She stayed at a hotel in Tokyo. Her room was 203 and the next room number was 205, not 204. She tried to find room 204 but she couldn't. She asked us why there was no room 204. My father answered, "Some Japanese think number four is a bad number. They don't like the number because it *is pronounced *the same as the word for *death. So, some hotels and hospitals don't have room numbers *ending in four in Japan." Diana said, "That's interesting. I didn't learn that in my Japanese class."

　　The next morning Diana and I got up and went to the living room. My parents were drinking green tea. Diana was a little surprised and said, "I thought Japanese people always drink green tea in a *special way." My mother said, "You are talking about a *tea ceremony but this is not a tea ceremony. We usually drink green tea as you drink tea or coffee."

In the afternoon, I took Diana to the summer festival in my town. A lot of people were walking through many kinds of shops along the street. Diana said, "Many girls are wearing kimonos. They are so beautiful. I learned that many years ago Japanese people *wore kimonos every day but today most people don't wear them. Why are those girls wearing kimonos today?" I answered, "They are wearing *yukata*, a kind of kimono. Many young girls like wearing *yukata* at summer festivals."

Before Diana left us we took her to a park near my house. We walked around and played on the *grass. Diana found a *four-leaf clover in the grass and said, "In my country it's a good thing to find a four-leaf clover. But it's really sad to find it on my last day with you, because four is a bad number in Japan." My father said to her, "Don't worry, Diana. Four-leaf clovers are good in Japan too." Diana said, "That's great. I'm happy now."

When we had to say good-bye to Diana, we gave her a present. I said, "You can open it now." Diana opened the present and said, "Oh, it's a *yukata*. I really like it. Thank you very much. I learned a lot about Japanese culture before I came here, and I thought I knew many things. But there are some things people don't know about a country *until they visit it. I've found out new things about Japanese culture. Three days are very short but staying with you has been more interesting than visiting some famous Japanese places."

*welcomed ～（～を歓迎した） is pronounced（発音される） the same as ～（～と同じように）
death（死） ending in ～（～で終わる） special way（特別な方法） tea ceremony（茶道）
wore ～（～を着ていた） grass（草地） four-leaf clover（四つ葉のクローバー） until ～（～まで）

本文の内容に合うように，次の英文に続けるのに最も適切なものを，**ア**～**エ**の中から１つ選びなさい。

Diana has found out

ア　that there are no hotels and hospitals in Tokyo.

イ　that she knows a lot about number four in Japan because she learned about Japan in her school.

ウ　that coffee is more popular than green tea in Japan today.

エ　that there are some things people don't know about a country until they visit it.

4 32% 次の英文を読んで，あとの問いに答えなさい。 〈青森県改題〉

　　*Jenny was eight years old and loved her grandmother. Jenny's house was *far from her grandmother's and they couldn't see each other often.

　　One day Jenny said, "*Dad, I want to have a birthday party for my *grandma. What do you think?" "That sounds great. There is a good restaurant near the station. It is called *'Lobster King.' I know the *owner well. Let's have a party there. I will *make a reservation for you." "Thank you, Dad."

　　Her father ran to the phone, called the restaurant and talked about the party to the *waiter.

> ＊Jenny（ジェニー） far（遠い） Dad（お父さん） grandma（おばあちゃん）
> 'Lobster King'（ロブスター・キング〈店名〉） owner（店主） make a reservation（予約する）
> waiter（ウェイター）

本文の内容と合うように，次の英文に続けるのに最も適切なものを，**ア〜エ**の中から一つ選びなさい。
Jenny's father ran to the phone
　ア　because he wanted to tell the waiter about the owner.
　イ　because he wanted to go to work soon.
　ウ　because he wanted to know what to do next.
　エ　because he wanted to help his *daughter.

＊daughter（娘）

5 22% 次の英文を読んで，あとの問いに答えなさい。 〈青森県〉

　　Long ago a *king lived in a small country and he was becoming old. One day he thought that he needed to find the next king. He wanted to find the best person to make his country better.

　　The king called all the young people in the country to the *palace. He said, "I will *choose the next king from you." The people there were surprised. He said, "I am going to give a *seed to everyone of you today. I want you to *plant it, give water to it and come back here six months from today with the *plant which will come from it. Then, I will look at the *plants and choose the next king."

　　It was exciting to the young people. *Joe was one of them. He went home and *planted it in a *pot very *carefully. Every day he gave water to it and watched it. After about two weeks some of the young people began to talk about their plants which came from their *seeds. Joe was sad to hear that. But he thought he needed more time and waited. Three months *passed, but Joe still didn't get any in his pot. He knew that his seed died.

　　Six months passed and the day came. Joe said to his mother, "I am not going to take my pot to the palace. People say the king will be *angry and *punish me when he looks at it." "What's wrong? I know you did the best thing you could. You must go and show it."

When Joe got to the palace, he was surprised to see the beautiful plants everyone brought *except him. When they saw his pot, they *laughed at him.

Then the king came. He walked around the room and said, "I'm very glad to see your plants. They show what kind of person you are." Then, he looked at a boy who had a pot with no plants and told him to come to the *front. Everyone worried about him.

The king said to the people, "Listen to me. Six months ago I gave everyone here a seed. But the seeds that I gave all of you *were boiled and I knew no plants came from them. All of you except this boy have beautiful plants now. That means you did something to get them. Look at his pot carefully. Can you see the plant in his pot? You can't! But this is the plant I wanted from the next king."

* king(王様) palace(宮殿) choose(～を選ぶ) seed(種) plant(～を植える) plant(植物)
plants(plant(植物)の複数形) Joe(ジョー〈人名〉) planted(plant(～を植える)の過去形) pot(鉢)
carefully(注意して) seeds(seed(種)の複数形) passed(～が過ぎた) angry(怒って)
punish(～を罰する) except(～以外の) laughed at(～を笑った) front(前)
were boiled(ゆでられていた)

本文の内容と合うように，次の英文に続けるのに最も適切なものを，ア～エの中から一つ選びなさい。

The king was very glad to see the plants the young people brought

ア　because the plants were useful and he found who was the best to be the new king.

イ　because from the plants he knew that many of them could be the new king.

ウ　because the plants made the palace beautiful and it was good for the country.

エ　because he found the best person to be the new king brought plants with flowers.

長文読解（絵や数字を読みとる）

例題

正答率
↓
49%

中学生の加奈（*Kana*）は，同じクラスの伸二（*Shinji*）から，アメリカにホームステイした時の話を聞いています。これを読んで，問いに答えなさい。

〈佐賀県改題〉

Shinji : Another example is that the bus carries your bike for you.

Kana : Really? It's very useful. How can you bring your bike into the bus?

Shinji : Well, you cannot bring it into the bus because there are many people, but you can put it on the front of the bus.

Kana : Oh, I see. It is easy to go around the city by bike and by bus.

下線部の内容を表した絵として最も適当なものを，次の**ア〜ウ**の中から一つ選び，記号を書きなさい。

ア　　　　　　　イ　　　　　　　ウ

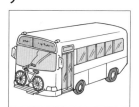  

ミスの傾向と対策　絵について説明している箇所は見つけやすいと思われるが，正答率は低かった。伸二の2つ目の発言にある on the front of の意味がわからなかったかもしれない。該当箇所の英文を注意深く読んで，その説明に合う絵を見極めよう。

解き方　下線部は「バスはあなたのために自転車を運ぶ」という意味。どのように運ぶかは，次の伸二の発言に注目。「バスの中に持ち込むことはできないが，バスの前にのせることができる」とあるので，これに合う絵は**ア**となる。

解答　ア

入試必出!　要点まとめ

Yuki is sitting <u>in front of</u> Mary.
└→「〜の前に」
「ユキはメアリーの前にすわっています」

● **英文に合う絵を選択する問題でよく使われる前置詞や連語**
- ・under 〜「〜の下に」　　・on 〜「〜の上に（接触して）」
- ・near 〜「〜の近くに」　　・by 〜「〜のそばに」
- ・between 〜 and …「〜と…の間に」
- ・among 〜「（3つ以上）の間に」

49% 次の対話文は，中学生の高也（Takaya）君と留学生のアン（Ann）さんが話をしているとき
のものです。あとの問いに答えなさい。　　　　　　　　　　　　　　　　　　　〈宮崎県〉

Takaya : Good morning, Ann. How are you?

Ann 　　: I'm fine, thank you. You look fine too, Takaya. Did you bring your
　　　　　 bento today?

Takaya : Yes, of course. Today is "*Bento-no-hi*."

Ann 　　: I know. Who made your *bento*?

Takaya : I did. I also made *bento* for my father today. How about you?

Ann 　　: I couldn't make *bento*. My host mother made it for me.

Takaya : I see. When *Bento-no-hi* started, I asked my mother to do it too.

Ann 　　: You didn't make your *bento* then, right?

Takaya : No, I didn't. Now I do. Our home economics teacher, Ms. Hama, often
　　　　　 tells us we should do more housework.

Ann 　　: Do you usually do other housework?

Takaya : I'm afraid not, but I try to do it when I can. Ms. Hama showed us a graph
　　　　　 that changed my mind about housework.

Ann 　　: What did the graph show?

Takaya : It showed how often the students in our school did housework.

Ann 　　: Sounds interesting. What facts did the graph show?

Takaya : Well, the largest number of students did housework almost every day. The
　　　　　 smallest number of students did no housework at all.

Ann 　　: Really? How about the others?

Takaya : The group of students who did some housework four times a week was
　　　　　 smaller than the group who did it once or twice a week.

Ann 　　: I see. The graph was surprising enough to change your mind, right?

Takaya : Yes, but I have another reason. I was moved by Ms. Hama's words. She
　　　　　 said, "We should do housework because we are a member of our family."

Ann 　　: That's for sure. Her words also move me. I'd like to start doing some
　　　　　 housework.

Takaya : Why don't you make your *bento* with your host mother on the next *Bento-
　　　　　 no-hi*?

　　　　　 * *bento*（弁当）　*Bento-no-hi*（弁当の日〈自分で作った弁当を持参して，会食する取り組み〉）

下線部a graph を表している最も適切なものを，次の**ア～エ**から１つ選び，記号で答えな
さい。

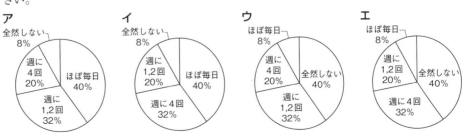

次の英文は，高志（Takashi）が，自分の関心のあるテーマについて，インターネットで調べてグラフ（graph）と表（table）を作り，英語の授業の時間に発表したときのものです。あとの問いに答えなさい。　　〈岐阜県〉

　　I've been interested in the environment since we studied about global warming. Last week, when I was looking for some information about the environment on the Internet, I found very interesting facts about forests. Today I'm going to talk about them.

　　First, look at the graph. This graph shows the *forest area percentages of Japan and four other countries. You can see that a high percentage of the land in Japan is forest area. Also, aren't you surprised to see that the forest area percentages of the other countries are lower? For example, look at the forest area percentage of _____. I thought that it would be over 50%, but the forest area percentage of _____ is about a half of the forest area percentage of Japan.

　　Now look at the table. This table shows ten *prefectures with the highest forest area percentages in Japan. You can see that only two prefectures have forest area percentages that are higher than 80%. Gifu is one of them.

　　I like Gifu very much because Gifu is *rich in nature. So, I hope that I can do something good for the environment in the future to take care of the forests in Gifu.

* forest area percentage(s)〈森林率〈ある地域の面積の中で森林面積が占める割合〉〉
prefecture(s)（県）　rich in nature（自然に恵まれた）

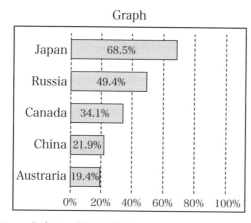

Graph

Japan	68.5%
Russia	49.4%
Canada	34.1%
China	21.9%
Austraria	19.4%

0%　20%　40%　60%　80%　100%

Table

Kochi	84.3%
Gifu	81.5%
Shimane	78.4%
Nagano	78.1%
Yamanashi	78.0%
Nara	77.1%
Wakayama	76.9%
Iwate	76.9%
Miyazaki	76.2%
Tokushima	75.3%

（グラフと表は，林野庁「森林・林業白書」をもとに作成）

本文中の _____ に入れるのに最も適切な国名を，次のア～エの中から一つ選び，その記号を書きなさい。
ア　Russia　　イ　Canada　　ウ　China　　エ　Australia

次の英文を読み，問いに答えなさい。　　　　　　　　　　　　　　　〈福島県〉

　Mark was a car *mechanic. He had a problem with his job. He didn't enjoy his job, because he *was tired of doing the same things every day.

　One day Mark got a letter from Japan. It was a letter from Ken. Mark thought, "I stayed in Japan for a month when I was fifteen. Ken was one of my friends. I haven't heard from him for ten years since then. What has happened?"

Dear Mark,

　Hello, this is Ken. Do you remember me? I am giving you another letter and a picture. The letter was written to you by yourself ten years ago. Do you remember Jiro, Keiko, you and I wrote letters to *ourselves to read ten years later? Last week the three of us enjoyed reading them. We talked about you and decided to send your letter and our picture to you.

　Now I want to write to you about us. I teach English in a high school. Thanks to you, I became very interested in English and studied it hard to be a teacher. I like teaching English. Jiro works as a barber. He enjoys talking with people while he is working. Keiko is a nurse. She says that her job is hard but a lot of fun. I hope you will write me soon.

Your friend,

Ken

---

　　　　　* mechanic（整備士）　was tired of 〜（〜に飽きていた）　ourselves（私たち自身）

本文の内容に合うように，次の　A　と　B　に入る最も適当な英語をそれぞれ書きなさい。数字も英語で書きなさい。

　When Mark was 　A　 years old, he got a letter from Ken for the 　B　 time after his stay in Japan.

長文読解（文や語の並べ替え・補充）

〈神奈川県改題〉

例題

正答率

46%

次の英文について，あとの問いに答えなさい。

　　I went to Kyoto last month. I visited many *temples there. The temple I liked the best was *Kinkaku-ji*. (　　) But I *was able to answer him. I was very happy.

* temples（寺）　was able to ～（～することができた）

英文中の（　　）の中に次の A～C の三つの文を入れるとき，A～C を並べる順番として最も適するものはどれか。

A. I was surprised because he suddenly talked to me in English.
B. One of them asked me about *Kinkaku-ji*.
C. When I went there, I saw many foreign people who were taking pictures.

ア　A→B→C　　イ　A→C→B　　ウ　B→A→C
エ　B→C→A　　オ　C→A→B　　カ　C→B→A

ミスの傾向と対策　　金閣寺を訪れたときの出来事を述べた文である。話の流れを順に追っていけば解きやすいが，正答率は低かった。代名詞が指すものを考えながら，文のつながりを考えて並べかえることができなかったのかもしれない。

解き方　　C にある there は空らんの直前にある *Kinkaku-ji* のこと。また，B にある one of them の them は，C の many foreign people を指す。また，A にある he は B の one of them を指す。したがって，C→B→A の順となる。

解答　カ

入試必出！ 要点まとめ

I went to **the park** this morning. There were **a lot of people** there.
　　　　　　　　　　　　　　　　　　　　　　　　　　└→the park を指す
Many of **them** were enjoying jogging.
　　　└→a lot of people を指す

「私は今朝公園へ行きました。そこにはたくさんの人がいました。彼らの多くはジョギングを楽しんでいました」

● **文を並べかえたり補充したりする問題では，代名詞や接続詞などに注目する。**
　代名詞 he〔she〕は前に出た 1 人の男性〔女性〕を指し，there「そこで〔に〕」は前に出た場所を表す語句を指す。また，文と文を結ぶ接続詞も，文を並べかえるときの手がかりとなる。and「そして」，but「でも」，so「それで，だから」などに注目しよう。

1 (46%)　次の英文を読んで，あとの問いに答えなさい。　　　　　　　　　　　〈新潟県〉

There is a man who started cleaning *toilets for his *company. He is the *president of the company.

About 50 years ago, the man started cleaning toilets for his company. He wanted all the *workers of his company to *do their best in their work. But some of the workers were tired and didn't feel happy, so their *manners were bad. At first the man didn't know what to say to them. 　a　 He knew that the office and the toilets in the company building were very *dirty. Then he thought, "The workers will feel happy if they can work in a *clean office." So he started to clean all the toilets in the company building *under this idea. Some of the workers were surprised and said, "Why is our president doing such a thing? He should do his work as president." But he still cleaned every day.

After a few months, some workers began to understand his idea. 　b　 They started to come early in the morning and helped him by cleaning all the toilets in the company building. Soon more workers started to help him. *Finally all of the workers cleaned the toilets together.

Then, the man started cleaning the toilets in the *public places near his company as a volunteer activity, and the people living near his company joined him. His volunteer activity made him very famous. 　c　

One day the man and the *members of his volunteer group were invited to a junior high school. They found that many of the toilets were dirty. Some of them were *broken. The teachers really wanted to make their school a happy place for every student. 　d　 So the man and the members of his volunteer group said to the teachers, "Cleaning toilets is important for making this school a happy place." And they taught the teachers and the students how to clean the toilets. Both the teachers and the students worked hard together. After a year, the school became very clean and the students felt happy. They became kind to *each other. No toilets were broken again.

Why can people change just by cleaning toilets? The man says, "You can feel happy when you are in a clean place. Cleaning toilets can make you kind because you can learn it is important to work together. Cleaning toilets can also make you strong because you need *energy to finish something you start. So let's clean toilets for other people, and for *yourself, too."

*toilet（トイレ）　company（会社）　president（社長）　worker（社員）　do their best（最善を尽くす）
manners（態度）　dirty（汚れている）　clean office（きれいな事務所）　under ～（～に基づいて）
finally（ついに）　public（公共の）　member（仲間）　broken（壊れている）　each other（お互い）
energy（活力）　yourself（あなた自身）

次の英文は，文中の　a　～　d　のどこに入れるのが最も適当か。当てはまる記号を書きなさい。

People from many places also started to do the volunteer activity with him.

2 **30%** 次の対話の文章を読んで，あとの問いに答えなさい。　　　　　〈東京都改題〉

Jasmine, a student from London, Mizuki, and Keisuke are talking in their classroom.
Their English teacher, Mr. Hara, has just come.

Mr. Hara	: Good morning, everyone. Jasmine, you look very happy today. Do you have any good news?
Jasmine	: Yes. I found my *muffler!
Keisuke	: <u>Oh, did you?</u> You lost it yesterday, right? Where was it?
Jasmine	: On a *mailbox near the station. I think someone *picked it up and put it there for me. It was *folded *neatly. I'm really happy because that muffler is very special to me. My mother made it and gave it to me when I left London. I'd like to tell that person my *feelings.
Mr. Hara	: That's good news. The person who put it there hoped that you would see it there.
Mizuki	: You're lucky, Jasmine. When I walk in the city, I sometimes see a baby shoe or a *glove put on a mailbox or on the *branch of a tree. I think such an *act is small. But I feel something warm and kind in it.
Keisuke	: Me, too. Such an act shows that the person has a kind heart.
Jasmine	: That's right. Our acts can sometimes show our feeling.
Keisuke	: I had an experience, too. Last Sunday I gave my seat to an old woman on a train, but I was so *shy that I couldn't speak. I stood up and gave her my seat. She smiled and said to me, "Thank you." I was very happy then. I said, "You're welcome." I agree, Jasmine.

* muffler（マフラー）　mailbox（ポスト）　pick ～ up（～を拾う）　fold（たたむ）　neatly（きちんと）
feelings（気持ち）　glove（手袋）　branch（枝）　act（行為）　shy（恥ずかしい）

下線部の Oh, did you? の内容を，次のように語句を補って書き表すとすれば，　　　の中
にどのような1語を入れるのがよいですか。

Oh, did you 　　　　　 your muffler?

3 45% シールド工法（shield method）について書かれた次の英文を読んで，あとの問いに答えな さい。　　　　　　　　　　　　　　　　　　　　　　　　　　　　　　　　　　　　〈栃木県〉

　　"London Bridge Is Falling Down" is a famous song about a bridge which fell down many times. This bridge was built over a big river that goes through London. In the 19th century, the river was very useful for *transporting things by *ship. Every day there were many big ships with *sails on the river. Many people gathered along rivers and built cities like London.

　　There was one problem. When ships went under the bridges, the sails hit the bridges. So, there were only a few bridges over the river. People couldn't go to the other side of it easily. 〔　ア　〕 Then, some people thought of an idea to build a *tunnel under the river. They made the tunnel with the "shield method." With this method, they could make a stronger tunnel because the tunnel was supported by *pipes called "shield" from the inside. Water didn't come into the tunnel, so the tunnel didn't break down easily. 〔　イ　〕

　　How did people find this way of building the tunnel? They found it from a small *creature's way of making a *hole in *wood. 〔　ウ　〕 At that time, ships were made of wood. The creatures called *Funakuimushi ate the wood of the ships and made some holes. When they eat wood, they put a special *liquid from its body on the wall of the hole. When this liquid becomes hard, the holes become strong. 〔　エ　〕 In this way, people found the way to make tunnels strong.

　　Today, around the world, there are many tunnels under the sea and in the mountains. A small creature gave us the idea to build strong tunnels. We may get a great idea from a small thing if we look at it carefully. By doing so, we can make better things.

　　　*transport（輸送する）　ship（船）　sail（帆）　tunnel（トンネル）　pipe（筒）　creature（生き物）
　　　hole（穴）　wood（木材）　*Funakuimushi*（フナクイムシ）　liquid（液体）

本文中の〔　ア　〕から〔　エ　〕のいずれかに次の１文が入る。最も適切な位 置はどれか。

People were so happy to have such a strong tunnel.

長文読解（英文の質問に英語で答える）

例題	次の文章を読んで，問いに答えなさい。〈千葉県〉

正答率

↓

46%

Masato, a high school student in Japan, went to Australia last summer to visit his friend Mark. He was interested in Australia and was *excited to visit another country for the first time. Mark lived in a big house in the *countryside, and it was very interesting to stay with him. Masato learned many things about life in Australia. For example, Mark's parents said, "In some *areas of Australia it hasn't rained a lot during *the last few years. So we must not use too much water." That *surprised Masato because in Japan it often rains. But Masato really understood their problem and decided that he would *take a short shower.

  * excited（わくわくした） countryside（田舎） area（地域） the last few years（ここ数年）
  surprise（～を驚かす） take a shower（シャワーを浴びる）

本文の内容に関する次の質問の答えを，次の**ア**～**エ**のうちから一つ選びなさい。

Why did Masato decide to take a short shower?

ア Because he learned parts of Australia didn't have enough rain for a few years.

イ Because he wanted Mark's parents to know it often rained in Japan last summer.

ウ Because he was surprised when Mark's parents asked him a problem.

エ Because he didn't know what problem people in Australia had.

ミスの傾向と対策	選択肢の英文が比較的難しく，また答えとなる文も本文とは異なる表現が用いられているので，低い正答率となったのかもしれない。本文の In some areas of Australia it hasn't rained a lot が正解の選択肢では parts of Australia didn't have enough rain と言いかえられているが，これが同じ内容であることがわからなかったのかもしれない。選択肢が本文の内容と合うか，1つ1つ検討しよう。

解き方	質問は「なぜマサトは短いシャワーを浴びることに決めたか」。第5，6文のマークの両親の言葉「オーストラリアのいくつかの地域では，ここ数年間あまり雨が降っていない。だから私たちは水を使いすぎてはいけない」より，**ア**の「彼はオーストラリアの一部では数年間十分な雨が降っていないと知ったから」が適切。

解答	**ア**

入試必出！ 要点まとめ

代名詞にする

Where did Tom go last Sunday? — He went to the library.

過去形にする 「図書館へ」

「どこへ」…場所を尋ねる疑問詞

「トムはこの前の日曜日にどこへ行きましたか」　「彼は図書館へ行きました」

● **質問の文と共通する語句を手がかりに，本文の該当箇所をさがす**
英文の質問に英語で答える問題で答えの文をさがすときは，質問の文と共通する語句を手がかりにすると，本文の該当箇所をさがしやすい。答えを書くときは，主語を代名詞にすることや，動詞の形に注意しよう。一般動詞を用いた，過去の疑問文に答えるときは，動詞を過去形にすることに注意しよう。

1 42%　次はフランク（Frank）と友人のロジャー（Roger）の対話文です。この対話文を読んで，あとの問いに答えなさい。　〈千葉県改題〉

Frank : Look! I've got four *tickets for the *Fancy Eagles *concert at *Aurora City Center!

Roger : Oh, my best friend! I can't wait to go!

Frank : Did I ask you to come with me?

Roger : Wait, Frank! We are best friends, right?

Frank : I'm just *joking! Let's go together. But you have to *pay for your own ticket.

Roger : Of course. I'll pay you tomorrow. But how did you get the tickets?

Frank : My father bought them when he saw the *poster yesterday. Please thank him.

Roger : Sure. I like your father! Did you ask Tim and Chris?

Frank : No. We only have four tickets.

Roger : What's the problem? If they go, there will be four of us.

Frank : Well, the poster says children under 17 have to go with a parent. We are only 16.

Roger : Oh, no! Did your father know about that?

Frank : I told him about it yesterday. I'm sure he can go with us. Now only one ticket is left.

Roger : Tim and Chris are best friends. We can't ask only one of them.

Frank : How about David or Daniel?

Roger : No, they always go to concerts together. How about Betty?

Frank : You mean the new girl from Canada?

Roger : Yes! Last week, she was talking to some students about her favorite *musicians. She has many favorite musicians, but she really loves the *Fancy Eagles*. She will be very happy if we ask her.

Frank : Good idea! Do you know her *phone number?

Roger : No, but it's OK. I can ask her tomorrow because we are in the same math class.

　　*ticket（入場券）　*Fancy Eagles*（ファンシー・イーグルス〈バンド名〉）　concert（コンサート）
　　Aurora City Center（オーロラシティーセンター〈施設名〉）　joke（冗談を言う）　pay（〈代金を〉支払う）
　　poster（ポスター）　musician（音楽家）　phone（電話）

本文の内容について，次の質問の答えとして最も適当なものを**ア**〜**エ**のうちから一つ選びなさい。

What is one problem Frank and Roger have?

ア　David and Daniel have never been to a concert before.

イ　They didn't know the *Fancy Eagles* concert *tour was *over.

ウ　They don't have enough tickets to invite two friends.

エ　Frank's father doesn't want them to pay for their tickets.

　　　　　　　*tour（ツアー）　over（終わって）

51

2 中学生のAkiraが書いた次の英文を読んで，あとの問いに答えなさい。　〈鹿児島県〉

　　This summer my friends and I went to a three-day event in my small town.　It was *planned by university students for junior high school students.　Many junior high school students from other towns joined, too.　The university students helped us with our studies.　We also played soccer and baseball with them.　Through these *activities, we made a lot of new friends.

　　People in my town helped with the event.　They *offered places for the activities.　They also cooked meals for us and the university students.　Some *elderly people told us about the town's history.　It was very interesting.　During those three days, people in my town looked very happy.

　　This event was a good *chance for us to make new friends and learn a lot from elderly people.　I hope this event will *be held again next year.

　　*Thanks to the university students, I had a good time this summer.　I want to plan events for my town in the future.　That's my dream.

> ＊plan ～（～を計画する）　activities（活動〈activityの複数形〉）　offered ～（～を提供した）
> elderly（年配の）　chance（機会）　be held（行われる）　Thanks to ～（～のおかげで）

次の〔1〕，〔2〕の質問に対する答えを英文で書きなさい。

41% 〔1〕Who planned this event?

35% 〔2〕What is Akira's dream?

---

3 次の文章を読んで，あとの問いに答えなさい。　〈千葉県〉

30%

　　Jane *went for a walk with her father in the morning.　When they came near the library, Jane stopped and said, "I haven't seen Shota for seven years, *Dad."　"You mean your first friend here in Japan?"　"Yes.　He lived near us, but he *moved away in the early summer when we were both eight."　"You *missed him very much when his family moved.　But why are you talking about him now?"　"It's the *lilies, Dad. We said good-bye in front of the lilies by his house.　They smelled very sweet at that time.　When I smell lilies, I always remember him."　Jane and her father looked back.　Some lilies were *giving off a sweet smell near the library.

> ＊go for a walk（散歩に行く）　Dad（父さん）　move away（引っ越す）
> miss（～がいなくなって寂しい）　lily（ゆり）　give off（～を放つ）

本文の内容に関する次の質問に，英語で答えなさい。

Where did Jane say good-bye to Shota?

次の英文は，中学生のヒロシ（Hiroshi）が自分の夢について書いたスピーチの原稿です。英文を読んで，あとの問いに答えなさい。 〈新潟県改題〉

Do you have a dream? I have one. I would like to talk about my dream.

There is a hospital near my house. When I become sick, I always go there to see a doctor. The doctor is Mr. Nojima. I like him because he is kind and teaches me many things. He is always kind to people who come to his hospital, so he is liked by them. He does three things when he sees his *patients.

First, when Mr. Nojima sees his patients, he asks them about their *hobbies. One day, when I became sick, I went to see him. He asked me, "What is your hobby?" I was surprised a little and said, "I like reading." Then, he said to me, "Who is your favorite *writer?" I told him the name of my favorite writer. One week later, I went to the hospital to see him again. When Mr. Nojima saw me, he smiled and said, "Oh, I read a book written by your favorite writer. It was a lot of fun." I was really surprised to hear that, and I became happy. Mr. Nojima said to me, "Having good communication with patients is the first *step when doctors see them. We must be interested in our patients." 〈後略〉

* patients（患者） hobby（趣味） writer（作家） step（一歩）

次の問いに対する答えを，3語以上の英文で書きなさい。

Why is Mr. Nojima liked by people who come to his hospital?

次の文章を読んで，あとの問いに答えなさい。 〈千葉県〉

One day, one of the students in my new class spoke to me for the first time. "I read your *poem in English class yesterday, Kevin. I like it very much." "Thanks ...," I said. "I've always felt *the same as you, but I didn't know how to *express *my feeling. I wanted to say that you expressed it *perfectly in your poem," she said. I was glad to hear that and asked, "Do you want to read other poems I wrote, Ellen?" Since that day, we have talked about poems a lot. And now we are good friends.

* poem（詩） the same as（～と同じように） express（～を表現する）
my feeling（私の感情） perfectly（完ぺきに）

本文の内容に関する次の質問に，英語で答えなさい。

How did Kevin feel when he heard Ellen's words?

次の英文は，高校生の高夫が，国境なき医師団（Doctors Without Borders）というNGO（非政府組織）について学んだあとに書いたものです。これを読んで，問いに答えなさい。

〈北海道〉

One day in an English lesson, Takao was *impressed with a story about Doctors Without Borders, an NGO which gives *medical treatment to people in countries with some problems. Also he learned many people want medical treatment from the NGO but the number of doctors is not enough. So more doctors are needed. After this lesson, Takao wanted to save people's *lives.

Takao talked about it with his father that night. Takao asked, "What should I do to be a member of Doctors Without Borders?" His father said, "First, you have to study a lot and enter a university for doctors. Another important thing is to learn how to *communicate with people from different countries." Takao felt he found the answer. He began to study harder at home and use English more during English lessons. Now Takao has a plan to go abroad after becoming a *medical student and hopes to study with students from other countries.

*impressed with（～に感動する）　medical treatment（治療）　life (lives)（生命）
communicate（コミュニケーションをとる）　medical student（医学生）

本文の内容から考えて，次の問いに対する答えを，主語と動詞を含む英文1文で書きなさい。
What did Takao start to do in English lessons after he talked with his father?

---

7 次の文章を読んで，あとの問いに答えなさい。　　　　　　　　　　　　　　　　　　〈東京都〉

Nobuyuki was a first-year student at a high school and a member of the Art Club. When he started high school, he began to think about becoming a professional *painter in the future.

One night, he said to his parents, "I want to study *painting at an art college after I finish high school." His mother thought that it would be good for him to do so. But his father was not a man who would say yes easily to that idea of his son's. His father said to Nobuyuki, "You don't understand that living as a professional painter is not easy."

Soon after Nobuyuki became a second-year student, he and other members of the Art Club started working very hard for an art contest in July. He said to his mother, "If I get a *prize, do you think Dad will understand my *feelings?" His mother said to him, "I'm sure he will."

One day in July, Mr. Yokoyama, an *advisor to the Art Club, received a letter from the office of the art contest. It *announced the *winners of prizes in the contest of that year. After classes on that day, Mr. Yokoyama called the names of the winners. He called Nobuyuki's name. That made Nobuyuki very happy.

That night, Nobuyuki told his parents about the contest. His father said to him, "It is great for you to get a prize, but you must think again about your future." When Nobuyuki heard this, he was *disappointed. After his father left the room, his mother said to him, "Don't be so disappointed. You really want to study art at college, right?"

In August, Nobuyuki visited his grandfather, Genzo, in a small village. He went there to paint mountains and a beautiful river. When Genzo saw his painting, he said to Nobuyuki, "You are a good painter, and your parents *are very proud of you." "No, my father never says good things about me," said Nobuyuki. Then Genzo said to Nobuyuki, "Well, I should tell you something about your father. Actually, he was really interested in painting at your age. He was just like you. But he knows that it's not easy to be a professional painter." Nobuyuki was surprised to hear that.

Then Genzo showed Nobuyuki a photo album and said, "This is an album your father gave me." Nobuyuki was very surprised to see a lot of photos of his paintings in the album. "I believe that your father is a big fan of yours. He has a *copy of the album, too," said Genzo. Nobuyuki learned that his father actually *cared about him very much. Genzo added, "Your father has wanted you to show him your *determination."

A week later, when Nobuyuki got back home, he talked to his father. Nobuyuki said to his father, "To be a professional painter has always been my dream. For my dream, I need to go to an art college." His father said to him, "If you promise that you will never give up your dream, I can give you a chance to go to one." Nobuyuki was very glad and promised that he would never do so.

One and a half years passed, and finally the day of the graduation ceremony arrived. Nobuyuki *was full of hope for a new life at an art college. His mother went to see the ceremony. His father didn't go there. After the ceremony, his mother gave Nobuyuki a letter from his father. It said, "Now, you're on the starting line." It was a very short message, but it made him happy.

*painter（画家） painting（絵画） prize（賞） feelings（気持ち） advisor（顧問）
announce（通知する） winner（受賞者） disappointed（がっかりした）
be proud of ～（～を誇りに思う） copy（同じもの） care about ～（～を気にかける）
determination（決意） be full of ～（～でいっぱいである）

次の質問に英語で答えなさい。

(31%) [1] Why did Nobuyuki visit his grandfather?

差がつく!!
(13%) [2] What did Nobuyuki promise when he talked about his future with his father?

次の英文は，高校生の結衣が，オーストラリアから来ていた留学生のルーシー（Lucy）のことについて書いたものです。これを読んで，あとの問いに答えなさい。　〈北海道〉

One day, I took Lucy to the *shogi* club in my school because she wanted to *experience some traditional Japanese culture. We watched the club members playing *shogi*. Lucy said to me, "Yui, *shogi* is cool because each *piece has some *kanji* on it." I said to Lucy, "*Shogi* is played by many people in Japan, and there are some famous *professional *shogi* players." （中略） "I also want to play *shogi*. Are the *rules of *shogi* difficult?" said Lucy. I said to her, "No. But first, you have to *remember how each piece moves." Lucy said she would try hard. Then she went to the club many times and learned the rules.

Last month, Lucy returned to Australia. I hear she is still interested in *shogi* and she plays it on the Internet because she wants to be a good player. I hope she'll keep playing it.

＊experience（経験する）　piece（〈将棋の〉駒）　professional（プロの）
rule(s)（ルール）　remember（覚える）

本文の内容から考えて，次の問いに対する答えを，主語と動詞を含む英文1文で書きなさい。
What does Lucy do to be a good *shogi* player?

9

次の英文は，バレーボール部に所属する中学生の早紀（Saki）が，転校生の恵子（Keiko）とのできごとを振り返って書いたものです。この英文を読んで，あとの問いに答えなさい。
〈静岡県〉

On the first day after the summer vacation, our class had a new student, Keiko. She stood in front of us and said, "Hello, my name is Keiko. Nice to meet you." Everyone in our class gave a warm *applause to Keiko. Then, she sat next to me.

In the short *break, I found that Keiko and I had the same *towel. So, my towel gave me a chance to speak to her. I said to her, "Look at my towel!" Keiko said, "Wow, the *character on our towels is my favorite!" Then, I asked Keiko about many things and both of us talked a lot together. When the break finished, I felt we were becoming friends. I thought, "I want to know more about Keiko."

The next day, I said to Keiko, "I'm on the volleyball team. What club were you in before?" Keiko said, "I was on the volleyball team, too." At that time, she tried to say something more, but she stopped saying the next words. I didn't know what she wanted to say and what club she wanted to be in, but I decided to invite her to the practice of our volleyball team. I said to her, "Why don't you practice volleyball with us after school?" She said, "OK." Keiko joined our practice on that day. She played volleyball well. In that week, she practiced with us two more days. We had a good time with Keiko and asked her to be on the volleyball team. But she didn't say anything about it.

On Monday of the next week, just before going to the gym, I said to Keiko, "You didn't join the volleyball practice yesterday. Will you join it today?" Then, she said, "Sorry, Saki. I won't practice volleyball." I asked, "Oh, why?" Keiko said, "Well ... I have something to do." She left the classroom quickly and didn't join the volleyball practice. When I was practicing volleyball, I thought only about Keiko.

The next morning, when Keiko came in the classroom, I spoke to her. I said, "Good morning. Well ... what did you do yesterday?" Keiko thought about what to say, and then she said, "I joined the practice of the *brass band. I want to be a *member of it." I asked, "Why didn't you tell me about that?" Keiko said, "My last school doesn't have the brass band, and I have never been in it. So, I'm not sure I will do well. Being a member of it will be a big *challenge." When I heard Keiko's words, I found the thing she wanted to try was different from the thing I wanted her to do. After school, I said to Keiko, "You should be in the brass band. You will get a good experience and learn something important. I hope you can do well!" Keiko looked glad to hear my words. She said, "OK ... I will try."

Now, Keiko is doing well in the brass band, and she is my best friend.

*applause（拍手） break（休憩） towel（タオル） character（キャラクター）
brass band（吹奏楽部） member（部員） challenge（挑戦）

次の質問に対して，英語で答えなさい。

 41% 〔1〕Why did Saki's towel give her a chance to speak to Keiko?

12% 〔2〕How many days did Keiko join the practice of the volleyball team?

長文読解（下線部の内容を答える）

例題

次の英文は，加奈が英語のスピーチコンテストで発表したときのものです。この英文を読んで，あとの問いに答えなさい。　　　　　　　　　〈宮城県改題〉

正答率
↓
46%

　Last month, my father taught me something interesting.
　One evening, he said, "How about spending two quiet hours without the lights from eight to ten? We will not watch TV, either."
　"No, I can't," I said. "I want to watch TV from eight to ten."
　"It's not good for you to watch TV too much," he said. "We need some time without the TV. And we will use *candles for our lights."

* candle(s)（ろうそく）

下線部について，加奈がそのように言った理由を，具体的に日本語で書きなさい。

ミスの傾向と対策　　　　下線部の直後に答えに該当する文があり，英文も複雑ではないと思われるが，正答率は比較的低かった。下線部の No, I can't, が表す内容をつかめなかったのかもしれない。直前の父親の言葉に注目して下線部中で省略された内容を考えよう。そして，下線部のあとにも注目して，理由が書かれている文をさがそう。

解き方　　　　下線部の「いいえ，できないわ」は直前の父親の言葉「8時から10時まで，明かりを消した静かな2時間を過ごすのはどうだろう。私たちはテレビも見ない」に答えたもの。その理由は直後の文で I want to watch TV from eight to ten. と説明されているので，これを日本語にして理由としてまとめる。

解答　（例）加奈は，8時から10時までテレビを見たかったから。

 入試必出！ ● **要点まとめ**

I learned **something important** from him. He said, "**We should help**
　　　　　　　　　　　　　　　　　　　　　　　　　↑
　　　　　　　　　　　　　　　　　　　　　下線部の具体的な内容を表す
each other to make this world better."

「私は彼から大切なことを学びました。彼は『私たちはこの世界をよりよくするために互いに助け合うべきだ』と言いました」

● **日本語で答えるときは，条件に合った答え方で答える**
　下線部の内容を日本語で答えるときは，設問文をよく読んで，条件などを確認して答えるようにしよう。字数制限がある場合はそれを必ず守ること。
　something important（大切なこと）のような，ことがらの内容を答える問題がよく出されるが，文末を「～こと」で終わるようにまとめよう。また，理由を答えるときは，文末を「～から〔ため／ので〕」にしよう。

33% 次の英文は，朝子（Asako）さんが「My dream」というタイトルで，英語の時間にスピーチをしたときの原稿です。問いに答えなさい。　〈宮崎県改題〉

Do you have a dream? If you have a dream, what is it? Is it going around the world? Is it becoming a *professional baseball player? Or is it becoming a writer? My dream is to become a *violinist.

I started to learn how to play the violin from my father when I was three years old. That means I've played the violin for twelve years. My father once said to me, "When you were three years old, your mother and I bought a violin for you. I belong to an *amateur orchestra in Miyazaki. My dream is to play the violin with you in the orchestra." My first dream was to join the amateur orchestra and play the violin with him. But I had a new dream when I was nine years old.

At that time, my parents took me to the Miyazaki Music Festival for the first time. The festival is now called *the Miyazaki International Music Festival. It is held every year and many people come to Miyazaki City from all over Japan. I still remember one *piece of the concert. It was a violin piece played by * Isaac Stern. He is famous as one of the greatest violinists in the world. It struck me the most. A lot of people who came to the Miyazaki Music Festival at that time were very impressed by it too. When I saw them, I really thought that a violin piece could make many people very happy. I decided to become a violinist like him. I know it is very difficult to become a violinist like him. When I worry about my dream, I remember my favorite book. It was written by Ichiro Suzuki, a famous professional baseball player. He says in the book, "You can't achieve your dream in one day. But, you will have an *unbelievable strength some day if you *keep on trying *steadily toward your dream." I love these words that help me a lot. I think that we can feel free to have our own dreams. He tells us there is one thing more important than having a dream. That is trying your best toward your dream. This year I will join the same amateur orchestra in Miyazaki that my father belongs to. My father's dream and my first dream will come true at last. After this I'll begin to achieve my next dream.

I want to ask you again. Do you have your own dream? If you have one, try your best to achieve your dream.

* professional（プロの）　violinist（バイオリニスト）　amateur orchestra（アマチュアのオーケストラ）
the Miyazaki International Music Festival（宮崎国際音楽祭）　piece（曲）
Isaac Stern（アイザック・スターン〈1920年〜2001年〉）　unbelievable strength（信じられない力）
keep on ～ing（～し続ける）　steadily（着実に）

本文中に下線部 I really thought that a violin piece could make many people very happy. とあるが，朝子さんがそのように思った理由を，本文の内容をふまえて，日本語で説明しなさい。

59

次はジュディ（*Judy*）とその母親サラ（*Sarah*）の会話の場面から始まる文章です。よく読んであとの問いに答えなさい。 〈長崎県〉

"Who is this boy?" Judy said to her mother, Sarah. Judy had a picture in her hand. "Oh, it's Hiroshi, my friend from Japan," Sarah said. It was Saturday afternoon. Judy was looking at her mother's old pictures. "He came to our town when I was in high school. He was an exchange student and stayed for one year. He was in my class and we had a good time together. I still have the letters he sent to me."

Sarah showed one of them to Judy.

Dear Sarah,

I left your town a month ago. How are you? I really enjoyed staying there. On the first day at school I was very *nervous, so I didn't talk much. When I was just sitting and didn't know what to do, you spoke to me and showed me around the school. After that day I made many new friends at school and learned many things. One day we talked about our dreams. When I said that I wanted to be an English teacher in Japan, you said to me, "That's wonderful! You can do it." <u>Do you remember?</u> Your words gave me hope. Now I'm studying hard for my dream. Please *say hello to your family and friends. I hope to see you again.

Your friend,

Hiroshi

* nervous（不安な）　say hello to ～（～によろしく言う）

下線部では，何について「覚えていますか」と尋ねているか。その内容を45字以上55字以内の日本語で書きなさい。なお，句読点も字数に含みます。

次の英文を読んで，問いに答えなさい。 〈栃木県〉

One Saturday, after Kenta played tennis at school, he went to a bookstore near his school. When he was looking for books, he saw a young woman *pushing a stroller on the *sidewalk. He found that she could not move because there were many bikes there. Kenta went out of the bookstore, and ran to the woman. He moved all the bikes away for her. She said, "Thank you. Tell me your name, please. You are a student at Minato Junior High School, aren't you?" "... Goodbye," Kenta said and ran away.

A few days later, at the classroom in the morning, Kenta was listening to his teacher. "Everyone, we got a letter from a woman yesterday. In the letter she says she was helped by a boy student of our school. When she was *in need near a bookstore, the boy was very kind to her. The boy didn't tell his name, so she sent the letter to our school to thank him. We're happy to get such a letter, and *we're proud of the good student." Kenta thought, "It's me, but (1)I'm not a good student."

After school, Kenta went to the teachers' room. He said to his teacher, "Excuse me. You told us about the letter from a woman this morning, didn't you? The student in that letter is me, but... I'm not a good boy. That day a lot of bikes were put on the sidewalk. I also put my bike there." Then, the teacher smiled at Kenta and said, "You put your bike on the sidewalk? That wasn't good, and you were *careless, weren't you? But you helped the woman in need. Most people want to help other people in need, but they usually don't. When you see people in need, I want you to help them." "OK, I will," Kenta said. When he was going to leave the room, his teacher said to him. "Kenta, if you are kind to others, they'll be happy and you'll be happy too. Please remember this."

The next week, Kenta had a tennis game in another town. After the game he took the bus to go home. There were not many people on the bus, so he took one of the *seats. He was a little tired and he *fell asleep. When he opened his eyes, the bus was full of people. Just then, an old woman got on the bus. Kenta stood up and gave his seat to her. The old woman thanked him and took the seat. When Kenta saw her smile, he became very happy. At that time, Kenta remembered (2)his teacher's words.

> * push a stroller（ベビーカーを押して動かす）　sidewalk（歩道）　in need（困っている）
> be proud of ～（～を誇りに思う）　careless（不注意な）　seat（座席）　fall asleep（眠り込む）

〔1〕 下線部（1）のように健太（Kenta）が思ったのはなぜか。日本語で書きなさい。 **30%**

〔2〕 下線部（2）の内容を日本語で書きなさい。 **37%**

4 次の英文は，里香（Rika）とリー（Lee）先生との対話の一部である。これを読んで，問い
に答えなさい。　　　　　　　　　　　　　　　　　　　　　　　　　　　〈栃木県改題〉

Rika : Hi, Mr. Lee. My friends and I chose a clock as a wedding present for Ms. Kato.

Mr. Lee : A clock? Why?

Rika : A new clock means a new life. We hope she starts a happy life.

Mr. Lee : Ms. Kato is glad to have wonderful students like you. By the way, it isn't good to send clocks in China. My mother once told me so.

Rika : Really? I didn't know that.

Mr. Lee : Well, I'll write two Chinese words. They mean different things. The first word means to send clocks to others. The second one means to take care of a sick person to the end of his or her life. But both of them have the same sound.

Rika : Oh, I understand. So, if you "send clocks" to people, they may think of "the end of life" and feel bad.

1	送	鐘
2	送	終

Mr. Lee : That's right. Also, my mother told me about an *umbrella. You should not give it to a *couple.

Rika : Umbrella? Why? When a couple share an umbrella, they look nice.

Mr. Lee : The Chinese words for "umbrella" and "*breaking up" have the same sound.

Rika : I am surprised. Good presents in one country are not good ones in another country.

Mr. Lee : That's right. When I send a present, I always think about one thing. I think how other people will feel when they get a present.

*umbrella（かさ）　couple（カップル）　breaking up（別れ）

下線部の指す内容を日本語で書きなさい。

次は，高校1年生のHiroshiが書いた作文です。これを読んで，あとの問いに答えなさい。

When I started high school, I thought it was difficult to do well in both sports and study. I love soccer and practice it hard almost every day. I want to play in *the World Cup. I also want to study English hard because I want to play soccer in other countries in the future. At first, doing both was not easy for me. When I went back home, I often went to bed early without studying because I practiced soccer so hard.

One day, I met a student from *Singapore. His name was Mark. He came to Japan through a *cultural exchange program with other students. They stayed for only a day at my school. Mark came to my English class. He also liked playing soccer, so we talked about it in English. It was fun to talk with him. When I talked with him in English, I didn't worry much about *making mistakes. I said, "You also practice soccer hard. Is it difficult to study hard too?" Mark said, "Yes, it is. But I try to *concentrate in class and ask the teachers when I don't understand something." We enjoyed talking about a lot of things. At the end of class, Mark said, "I'm glad I talked with you. Let's send e-mails to each other in English." I thought it was a good idea and agreed.

I had to write my e-mail in English, so I started to study English harder. I first concentrated more in my English class. I began to understand it better than before, but I also needed time to *review. I easily found time to study on the weekend, but from Monday to Friday, I often went to bed early because I practiced soccer so hard. This was a problem. One evening, I talked about this with my father. He said, "I also have to study English because I need it for my work. I often come home late, so it is difficult to study at night. I get up early *instead and study before I go to work. I try to use my time *effectively. You practice soccer every day because you want to be a better soccer player. If you want to make your English better, you should study English every day too. I often see some high school students who are studying on the early morning train." From the next day, I tried to get up early like my father.

Now I study English every morning. This has become the most important thing for making my English better. I also leave home earlier than before. I usually get on the train that my father takes. I often see high school students, and some of them are studying for class. My father's words were true. I also started reading my textbooks on the train.

I received an e-mail from Mark. In his e-mail, he said that he studied math hard. I sent an e-mail back. In my e-mail, I said, "I make time to study English at home before I go to school. It is not easy to do well in both soccer and English, but I'll never give up."

 * the World Cup (〈サッカーの〉ワールドカップ)　Singapore (シンガポール)
 cultural exchange program (文化交流プログラム)　make a mistake (間違いをする)
 concentrate (集中する)　review (復習する)　instead (その代わりに)　effectively (有効に)

HiroshiがMy father's words were true.と書いたmy father's wordsの具体的な内容はどのようなことか。日本語で書きなさい。

長文読解（指示語の内容を答える）

例題

正答率

43%

次の英文を読んで，問いに答えなさい。　　　　　　　　　　　〈栃木県改題〉

　　As you know, we have six kinds of *coins in Japan. They are 1, 5, 10, 50, 100 and 500 yen coins. We see them *almost every day, but can you remember their *designs? Let's think about some coins. On 10 yen coins, there is a very famous building. On 100 yen coins, there are *cherry blossoms. By the way, have you ever thought about what each design means? It is very interesting to study <u>it</u> because we can learn something about Japan.

　　*coin（硬貨）　almost（ほとんど）　design（デザイン）　cherry blossoms（桜）

下線部 it の指すものを本文中から英語４語で抜き出しなさい。

ミスの傾向と対策　　it が指すものを本文中から４語で抜き出す問題だが，正答率があまり高くなかった。it が単なる名詞ではなく，what で始まる間接疑問を指していることを見抜けなかったのかもしれない。指示語の内容を答える問題では，まず指示語〔代名詞〕が単数のものを指すか複数のものを指すかを判断し，前の部分に注目してさがすようにしよう。

解き方　　it は前に出た単数のものだけでなく，文の内容の一部も表せる。「私たちは日本について何か学べるので，それを勉強することはとてもおもしろい」の「それ」は，直前の文に「あなたは今までにそれぞれのデザインが何を意味するかについて考えたことがありますか」とあるので，it は what each design means を指すとわかる。

解答　　what each design means

　**要点まとめ**

I read **a book** yesterday. **It** had **many short stories**. **They** were very

　　　　　　　　a book を指す　　　　　　　　　　many short stories を指す

interesting.

「私はきのう本を読みました。それには短い物語がたくさんありました。それらはとてもおもしろかったです」

● **代名詞 it, they, them が指すもの**

①it…前に出た単数のものや文の内容などを指す。

　I have a computer. It is very useful. I use it every day.

　「私はコンピュータを持っている。それはとても便利だ。私はそれを毎日使っている」

②they, them…前に出た複数の人〔もの〕を指す。

　I have two brothers. They are high school students. I like them very much.

　「私には２人の兄弟がいる。彼らは高校生だ。私は彼らが大好きだ」

 40% 次の英文を読んで、あとの問いに答えなさい。 〈広島県〉

A high school student Tatsuya went to a town in *England to stay with the Davis family last spring. In the family, there were Mr. Davis, Mrs. Davis and their child, Mike. He was eleven years old.

One day at dinner time Tatsuya said, "I've brought many pictures I took in Japan. I'll show them to you later." Mike said, "Really? That will be interesting." After dinner Tatsuya showed the pictures to the family. Mike looked at the first picture and said, "Tatsuya, these flowers look very beautiful. What are <u>they</u>?" Tatsuya answered, "They are *cherry blossoms. We enjoy watching them at this season of the year." Mrs. Davis looked at another picture and said, "I feel *peaceful to see this picture. What's this?" Tatsuya said to her, "It's my favorite Japanese garden. Large and small *rocks are *arranged well on white *sand here. Many people visit this garden and feel peaceful."

Mike said, "Oh, is it a garden? I've never seen such a garden in England." Then Mr. Davis said, "Let's go to see a *historic building in *Kent next weekend. It has beautiful gardens." Tatsuya said, "That sounds great! I want to take pictures of *English gardens." Mr. Davis said, "We can get to the place by train and bus. From the train we can enjoy a nice *landscape of England." The Davis family enjoyed Tatsuya's pictures very much that night.

＊England（イングランド〈英国の一部〉） cherry blossom（桜の花） peaceful（安らかな） rock（岩）
arrange（配置する） sand（砂） historic（歴史的な） Kent（ケント〈イングランドの州〉）
English（イングランドの） landscape（景色）

本文中の they は何を指しているか。本文中から抜き出して書きなさい。

次の英文は，シンガポール（Singapore）を旅行中の真二（Shinji）と，現地の女性との対話の一部です。これを読んで，問いに答えなさい。 〈栃木県改題〉

Woman : Excuse me, are you a *tourist? Please stop drinking!

Shinji : Why? It's very hot today, so I just want to drink this water.

Woman : You can't eat or drink on the train. If you <u>do so</u>, you have to *pay a lot of money. In Singapore, we have our own rules.

Shinji : Oh, I didn't know that.

Woman : You have just learned one of the rules.

Shinji : Yes. Thank you very much. What other rules do you have?

Woman : For example, we can't pick up flowers, or give food to birds in the park. If people do those things in Singapore, they have to pay a lot of money.

Shinji : Umm..., I think the rules are very strict.

Woman : You're right, but we accept them, and try to make a more beautiful country. We want many foreign people to come here.

Shinji : I see. People in Singapore really love this beautiful country.

* tourist（観光客） pay（払う）

下線部の指す内容を日本語で書きなさい。

There are a lot of people around us. Some people have the *same ideas and other people have different ones. Is it difficult to be friends with people who have different ideas? Animals may have some answers to this question.

People have been good friends with some animals for a long time. Some people have animals at home as their pets. A lot of children like to go to a zoo to see animals.

Some people say, "Animals sometimes look like people." Do you agree? Other people say, "Animals can feel sad and love other animals, too." Do you believe it? You may not believe it but there are some examples.

For example, a dog is happy and *moves its *tail fast when its *owner comes home and is happy to see the dog. Have you ever seen a cat that comes to its owner and tries to *cheer its owner up when the owner is crying? How about a dog that looks sad when its owner is sad? These are some of the examples which show that animals share *feelings with people.

*same（同じ） move ～（～を動かす） tail（尾） owner（飼い主）
cheer ～ up（～を元気づける） feelings（感情）

下線部分について，その内容を三つ，具体的に日本語で書きなさい。

次の英文は，中学生の晴樹（Haruki）が書いたスピーチ原稿です。これを読んで，あとの
問いに答えなさい。　　　　　　　　　　　　　　　　　　　　　　　　　　　〈宮崎県改題〉

"Good morning, Haruki."

This cheerful greeting from Mr. Yamamoto gives me the power to start the day.
He is a 68-year-old man who lives near my house. He *retired from his job 8 years
ago. Since then, he has watched students on their way to school as a volunteer every
day. He is a part of our community.

One morning in May, Mr. Yamamoto asked, "Are you busy with soccer
practice?" I was on the soccer team at school. I said, "Yes. I practice it very hard
every day. The last local tournament will come soon. I'll be glad if you can come
and watch the games." He said with a *smile, "Of course."

On that night, my father came back home early. I enjoyed dinner with my
family. In April, he was so busy with his work that he didn't come home early.
During the dinner, I talked a lot about my school life such as friends, club activities
and Mr. Yamamoto. I also asked my father to come to the tournament. Suddenly, he
stopped eating his dinner. After several seconds, he said, "Haruki, I really want to
see your games, but I can't. I have a very important meeting. I want to go ...." He
was still trying to say something. Then I stood up and said to him, "You always
came to my soccer games before. This time, you won't come. Why not? This is
my last tournament. Your work must be more important for you than me." I went to
my room and closed the door.

The next morning, "What happened, Haruki? You look sad," Mr. Yamamoto
asked me gently. I talked about the story from the last night. After I finished
talking, he said, "I know how you feel, but at the same time, I know how your father
feels. Your father always thinks about you." I asked, "Why can you say that?" He
said, "My son and I had a similar experience 20 years ago." I was surprised and
asked, "Oh, did you?" He said, "Yes. I was also busy like your dad and never went
to see my son's baseball games. I was very sorry for <u>that</u>. But there were many
kind people in this community. They cared about my son very much, so he said he
didn't feel sad. After this experience, I decided to work hard for my neighbors some
day. Now, I am happy to help you this way in your father's place. You are not
alone!"

Through his words, I understood my father's *feelings. He never thought his
work was more important than me. I also learned I was helped by many people in
my community. I decided to share this story with my father by writing a letter.

In the end, my father couldn't come to my last tournament but I didn't feel sad.
Now, I am thinking about the way to make my neighbors happy. This is an
important step to be a good member of our community like Mr. Yamamoto.

　　　　　　　　　　　　　　　　* retire（退職する）　smile（笑顔）　feeling（感情）

文中の下線部 that が指している内容を，30字以内の日本語で答えなさい。

5 修と留学生のメアリーが，わさび（*wasabi*）について次のような会話をしています。この英文を読んで，あとの問いに答えなさい。

〈宮城県改題〉

Mary : When I was watching a *TV program about Japanese food, I saw a green food. People were eating *sashimi* with it. Do you know what it is?

Osamu : I think it is *wasabi*. As you know, Japan is an island country, so Japanese people eat a lot of fish from the sea. We eat *sashimi* with *soy sauce and *wasabi*. *Wasabi* is very *hot, but it *tastes good.

Mary : I think soy sauce tastes good. Does *wasabi* taste good, too?

Osamu : Yes, it does. I like it very much. For example, I eat *sushi*, *soba* and *ochazuke* with *wasabi*. Sometimes, some people eat it with *miso* and *mayonnaise, and others eat *steak with it.

Mary : *Wasabi* is very popular among Japanese people, right?

Osamu : Yes. And my father told me an interesting story about *wasabi*.

Mary : What did he say?

Osamu : About 400 years ago, Japanese people already knew that *wasabi* and soy sauce could make food *delicious. At that time, they started to eat *sushi* and *soba*, and they started to *grow *wasabi* and to make soy sauce. My father also said there was another good thing about using *wasabi*.

Mary : What was that?

Osamu : *A long time ago, *wasabi* was used as a kind of *medicinal herb because it can *kill bacteria. Today many Japanese people eat *wasabi* with many kinds of food, but some Japanese people may not know about <u>this</u>.

Mary : I understand *wasabi* is eaten by many people. I want to try it and I will write a letter to my friends in America about it.

Osamu : I hope they will like *wasabi* if they try it. I also hope *wasabi* will become as popular as soy sauce there.

＊TV program（テレビ番組） soy sauce（しょう油） hot（からい） tastes（＜taste 味がする）
mayonnaise（マヨネーズ） steak（ステーキ） delicious（おいしい） grow（栽培する）
a long time ago（昔） medicinal herb（薬草） kill bacteria（細菌を殺す）

下線部の this の示す内容を，具体的に日本語で書きなさい。

例題

次の英文は，和子が将来の夢について書いたものの一部です。これを読んで，問いに答えなさい。　　　　　　　　　　　〈北海道改題〉

正答率
↓
49%

　　That evening, when we were enjoying the cake we bought from the shop, my mother said, "You looked so interested when you were talking with the young woman. How about becoming a *pâtissier?"

　　I said, "I'm interested in making *sweets, but I haven't decided what to become."

　　Then, my father gave me some *advice. "Kazuko, when you think about your job, remember these three things. I hope they'll help you. First, you must *become independent of us. That means you must live *by yourself. Second, you'll be happy if you *fulfill your dream by getting your job. Third, this is the most important, I think your job should make other people happy." I said, "Thank you, Father. I'll try."

* pâtissier (ケーキ職人，パティシエ)　sweet(s) (〈ケーキなどの〉菓子)　advice (アドバイス)
become independent of (〜からひとり立ちする)　by oneself (自分の力で)　fulfill (かなえる)

父親が和子に話した3つのアドバイスのうちから1つを選び，その内容を日本語で書きなさい。

**ミスの
傾向と対策**　　設問文にある「3つのアドバイス」をヒントにすれば，該当箇所は見つけやすいと思われるが，正答率はあまり高くなかった。該当箇所の3つの英文のうち1つを答えればよいので，訳しやすいものを選んで答えよう。また，「アドバイス」を答えるので，文末を「〜こと」にするなど，答え方にも気をつけよう。

解き方　　第3段落の　〜, remember these three things「これらの3つのことを覚えておきなさい」に注目する。このあとの First, Second, Third で始まる3文が，父親が和子に話した3つのアドバイスなので，この中の1つを答える。

解答　　（例）親からひとり立ちしなければならないということ。〔自分の力で生活していかなくてはならないということ。〕／仕事につくことで自分の夢をかなえられたら，幸せだろうということ。／自分の仕事が，他の人々を幸福にするべきだということ。

入試必出！ 要点まとめ

I want to be an astronaut.　That's my dream.
「私は宇宙飛行士になりたいです。それが私の夢です」

● **設問文のキーワードを手がかりに該当箇所をさがす**
　　下線部がない問題では，本文全体から該当箇所をさがさなければならない。設問文からキーワードを見つけてそれを手がかりにすれば，早く該当箇所が見つかる。「驚いたのはなぜか」という設問なら be surprised を，「〜の夢は何か」という設問なら，dream「夢」をキーワードにして，それが出てくる箇所の前後をさがせば，答えが見つかるはずだ。

次の文章を読んで，あとの問いに答えなさい。　　　　　　　　〈福岡県〉

Yuko is a high school student in Fukuoka now. She is a member of the *taiko* team in her town. She started to play the *taiko* when she was a junior high school student.

Three years ago, she went to Nara and Kyoto on a school trip. She visited a lot of famous places and listened to old Japanese music.

She saw some *taiko* teams and became interested in old Japanese music then. She wanted to know more about *taiko*, so she used the Internet and found a *taiko* team in her town.

A few days later, Yuko went to see the *taiko* team after school. The team had about twenty members. Some of them were younger than Yuko. Mr. Yamamoto, the oldest one on the team, was seventy years old. He lived in this town for a long time. The members looked happy when they were playing the *taiko*. The sound of the *taiko* was very exciting to Yuko. She asked Mr. Yamamoto, "How long have you played the *taiko*?" He answered, "I've played it for about sixty years." "Why have you played it for such a long time?" she asked. He answered, "Because it has been my favorite thing *since I was nine years old. We have played the *taiko* in this town for many years. Playing the *taiko* is important to our culture. I think we should *continue this tradition for the people living in this town."

After listening to his words, she was surprised and said, "You've done useful things for our town. I want to be like you."

Then Mr. Yamamoto said to her, "Why don't you join our team?"

She smiled and answered, "Sure, I want to play the *taiko* with the team for the people who live in this town too."

* since ~（～以来）　continue this tradition（この伝統を守る）

裕子（Yuko）は，山本さん（Mr. Yamamoto）の言葉を聞いたあと，驚いて何と言ったか。その内容を本文中からさがし，日本語で書きなさい。

次の英文を読んで，あとの問いに答えなさい。 〈新潟県〉

　　The *following story is one of the examples which shows a good *relationship between two different kinds of animals. It is about a *bear and a cat at a zoo.

　　The bear was born in the zoo and lived there *throughout its life. One day, a cat came to the zoo. No one knew where the cat came from. The cat went into the bear's *cage. When the cat and the bear saw each other, the cat walked to the bear. The cat wasn't afraid of the bear and the bear didn't *attack the cat. They became friends. They ate the *same food together. They slept together. People were surprised to see the relationship between the big animal and the small animal. One of the workers at the zoo said, "It's not *usual to see such a good relationship between two different kinds of animals. People who visit this zoo like watching them."

　　One day the bear was *moved from its cage. The cage was old and the workers had to *repair it. After the bear was moved to a place in a building, the cat walked around the cage and looked for the bear but it couldn't find its friend. Finally, the workers finished repairing the cage and they moved the bear to the new cage. The cat also came to the cage. The cat could go into the cage and go out of it again. The bear and the cat had a good time together again, so they looked happy.

　　You may not believe that these two different kinds of animals became such good friends. We don't know why the bear and the cat had a happy time together without *fighting, but it is important to try to learn something from these animals. Different kinds of animals can live *happily together. So we can also live happily together with a lot of people in the world. You may think it is not easy because some people have different ideas and other people speak different languages. To have good relationships with them, we should try to understand each other and to share our ideas. I hope we can live happily together like the bear and the cat.

> *following（次の）　relationship（関係）　bear（クマ）　throughout ～（～の間ずっと）
> cage（おり）　attack ～（～を襲う）　same（同じ）　usual（普通の）
> move ～（～を動かす）　repair ～（～を直す）　fighting（争い）　happily（幸せに）

文中では，さまざまな人々とよい関係を持つためには，どうすべきであると述べられているか。具体的に日本語で書きなさい。

次の英文を読んで，あとの問いに答えなさい。 〈埼玉県〉

　　Mayumi and Ayako are students at Nishi Junior High School, and they are good friends. One day in May they met at the station to do some shopping. They saw a new building by the station and some new shops on the first floor. They also saw that there weren't any more cherry trees in front of the station. Mayumi said, "Shopping at the new stores will be fun, but...." Ayako said, "We can't see the cherry blossoms next year."

A few days later, when Mayumi and Ayako were on their way home from school, they saw that some trees were *cut down in a small forest. They stopped walking, and then Mayumi said, "On the way to school this morning, these trees were a part of the small forest." Ayako said, "Today someone cut down these trees. I think more trees will be cut down." Mayumi said, "I think so too." She almost cried. She remembered seeing the beautiful trees in spring, *catching insects in summer and *picking up acorns in fall with Ayako and other friends. She liked the small forest very much.

The next day Mayumi talked to Mr. Ogawa at school. He was her science teacher. She talked to him about the cherry trees and the small forest. Mr. Ogawa understood how she felt. He said, "I think there are some *reasons for cutting down trees." Then he told her about the ideas of *sustainable *development and a sustainable *society. He thought she would be interested in them. She asked him to tell her more. He said, "Development is needed, but we also need to think about the environment for our future and our children's future." Mayumi thought it was a good idea, but she didn't know what to do. He said, "We should keep thinking about a sustainable society. We also should do something for the environment. There are many easy things we can do for the environment. For example, we can *turn off switches to *conserve electricity. Also I'm *growing *morning glories to make a *green curtain. You should begin with easy things you can do for the environment." She became interested.

After school Mayumi and Ayako went back home together. Mayumi told Ayako about talking with Mr. Ogawa. Ayako asked, "What is a green curtain?" Mayumi answered, "A green curtain *makes shade with plants like morning glories. It can make rooms cooler in summer, so we can conserve electricity." Ayako said, "I want to make green curtains at my house." Mayumi said, "Me too. Tomorrow let's talk about green curtains with our classmates. I want to make them at school too." Ayako said, "That's a good idea. Our classmates will like our ideas." Then Ayako told Mayumi about last night's TV news. Ayako said, "Some volunteers were *planting young trees by the river. I want to do volunteer work when I start high school." Mayumi thought that was a good idea too, so she said, "When we start high school, let's do something for the environment as volunteers and learn more about it." Ayako said, "Let's do it!"

*cut（cut ～（～を切る）の過去分詞形）　catch insects（虫をつかまえる）
pick up acorns（どんぐりを拾う）　reason（理由）　sustainable（持続可能な）
development（開発）　society（社会）　turn off switches（スイッチを切る）
conserve electricity（電気を節約する）　grow ～（～を育てる）　morning glory（アサガオ）
green curtain（緑のカーテン，グリーンカーテン）　make shade with plants（植物で日かげをつくる）
plant ～（～を植える）

Mayumi と Ayako は，高校に進学してどのようなことをしてみたいと述べているか。日本語で書きなさい。

長文読解（本文の内容と合うものを選ぶ）

例題

正答率
↓

49%

次の英文の内容と合っているものを，**ア～エ**から一つ選びなさい。〈秋田県改題〉

 Judy loves music. Yesterday she went to a concert to listen to her favorite singer. The singer sang only his new songs. After the concert Judy said to her friends, "I really wanted to listen to his old songs too."

ア Judy couldn't go to the singer's concert.
イ Judy enjoyed the singer's new songs and old songs at the concert.
ウ Judy went to the singer's concert just to listen to the singer's new songs.
エ Judy wanted to listen to the singer's old songs at the concert too, but she couldn't.

ミスの傾向と対策

 英文は短いので内容はつかみやすいと思われるが，正答率が低かった。この英文のポイントとなる「その歌手は彼の新しい歌しか歌わなかった」という内容がしっかりつかめなかったのかもしれない。各選択肢の意味を正しくとらえて，英文の内容と合っているか1つ1つ検討しよう。

解き方

 第3・4文に「その歌手は彼の新しい歌しか歌わなかった」「私（＝ジュディ）は彼の古い歌も本当に聴きたかった」とあるので，**エ**の「ジュディはコンサートでその歌手の古い歌も聴きたかったが，聴けなかった」が適切。**ア**は第2文，**イ**は第3文の内容と合わない。**ウ**は，コンサートに行った目的を表すjust to ～「単に～するために，～するためだけに」の部分が第4文の内容と合わない。

解答 **エ**

 **要点まとめ**

Mary called Bill **to ask** him about her homework.
     「～するために」…目的を表す
「メアリーは宿題について尋ねるためにビルに電話をかけました」

● **選択肢と本文を照らし合わせて違いを見つける**
本文の内容と合うものを選ぶ問題では，選択肢の英文と本文を注意深く照らし合わせて，内容が合っているかどうか確認することが大切。「だれが，いつ，どこで，どういう目的で，何をしたか」にポイントをおいて，本文と照合しよう。本文との違いを見つけたら消去法で消していき，残ったものも本当に正しいかどうか，もう一度確認しよう。選択肢では本文の内容が別の表現で言いかえられている場合も多いので，英文の内容をしっかりつかもう。

1 (42%) 次の英文は，洋子と，隣に引っ越しをしてきたビルの会話です。この英文を読んで，あと の問いに答えなさい。 〈宮城県改題〉

Bill : Hello, nice to meet you. My name is Bill, and I moved in *next door yesterday. So, I came here to say hello to your family.

Yoko : Oh, nice to meet you, too. My name is Yoko. Thank you for coming. Are you a high school student?

Bill : Yes, I will go to Miyagi High School from next Monday.

Yoko : Wow, that's my school. You and I will be students at the same high school. And where are you from?

Bill : I came from New York with my parents. My father will work at a *factory near here. So I had to leave my city and I feel a little sad now.

Yoko : I understand how you feel, but you will have a good time in this town.

Bill : Thank you. I am happy to hear that.

Yoko : Do you have any questions?

Bill : Yes. How do you go to school?

Yoko : I usually go there by bike. It takes about fifteen minutes from here. But I take a bus when it rains.

Bill : I see. I think riding a bike is the best *way to go to school. I will buy one this *weekend. Does the bus come very often?

Yoko : Yes, in the morning, it comes every ten minutes. If you take a bus, I will go with you.

Bill : Thank you very much. See you next Monday.

Yoko : See you.

＊next door（隣） factory（工場） way（方法） weekend（週末）

本文の内容に合う英文を，次の**ア**〜**オ**の中から２つ選びなさい。

ア Bill visited Yoko's house to say hello to her family.

イ Bill will work at a factory near here.

ウ Yoko usually walks to school from her house.

エ Yoko and Bill can take a bus every ten minutes all day.

オ Yoko will see Bill next week.

次の英文の内容と合っているものを，**ア〜エ**から一つ選びなさい。　　　　　〈秋田県改題〉

　　　　Tom likes to watch soccer games on TV.　Yesterday he couldn't watch a big game because he was busy.　Then he remembered his friend Emily.　She is also a big fan of soccer and always *records soccer games.　So he called her and asked, "Did you record the game?"

*record〜（〜を録画する）

ア　Tom called Emily to invite her to the big game.
イ　Tom called Emily to get her help with yesterday's big game.
ウ　Tom called Emily to ask her to be a big fan of soccer like him.
エ　Tom called Emily to talk about yesterday's big game he watched.

次の英文は，高校生の香奈が，ハワイから来た留学生のオリビア（Olivia）と，教室で会話している場面のものです。これを読んで，問いに答えなさい。　　　　〈北海道〉

Olivia : What did you do last weekend?
Kana : I went to the *beach with my family.
Olivia : Did you enjoy it?
Kana : Yes, I did.　But the beach we visited wasn't clean, so after having lunch, we cleaned it and collected many *plastic bottles and *plastic bags there.
Olivia : Oh, I also cleaned a beach and collected them with my friends in Hawaii last year.　The *letters on some of them were written in Japanese.　I was surprised because they traveled so far.
Kana : I think *plastic garbage is a problem around the world.
Olivia : I think so, too.　It doesn't *disappear naturally from the beaches and the sea.　It's bad for the environment.
Kana : I read an *article in a magazine about other problems of plastic garbage.
Olivia : Really?　Will you tell me about the article?
Kana : Sure.　Many animals in the sea eat plastic garbage because they think it's food.　Then, they can't *digest it and won't eat any more food.
Olivia : And many of them die, right?
Kana : Yes.　So we must *reduce plastic garbage.　I heard some Japanese high school students are trying to clean the sea with *fishers.　They collect garbage from the bottom of the sea, and then the students tell the world about the *action.　I also heard there's much plastic garbage in it.
Olivia : I think it's difficult for us to do it with fishers right now, but we should start reducing plastic garbage.　Kana, what can we do?
Kana : We can bring our own *canteens to school and take our own bags for shopping.
Olivia : That's good.　I think these actions are small, but it's important for us to do

good things for the environment.

Kana : That's right. If many high school students do it to reduce plastic garbage, the environment of the beaches and the sea will be good. So let's start talking about the problems with our friends first!

Olivia : OK!

＊ beach(es)（ビーチ） plastic bottle(s)（ペットボトル） plastic bag(s)（ポリ袋，ビニール袋） letter(s)（文字） plastic garbage（プラスチックごみ） disappear naturally（自然に消える） article（記事） digest（消化する） reduce（減らす） fisher(s)（漁師） action(s)（行動） canteen(s)（水筒）

本文の内容に合うものを，**ア**〜**オ**から 2 つ選びなさい。

ア Kana and her family cleaned the beach after they ate lunch.

イ Olivia hasn't collected plastic garbage with her friends yet.

ウ Kana read an article about Japanese garbage which is traveling so far.

エ Some high school students in Hawaii cleaned the sea with fishers.

オ Kana and Olivia decided to talk about the problems with their friends.

次の文章を読んで，本文の内容と合っているものをあとの**ア**〜**エ**のうちから一つ選びなさい。

〈千葉県改題〉

Tim is an *ALT from Australia. *On his first visit to Kyoto, his friends said that he should see *Kinkaku-ji, the Golden Temple, and *Ginkaku-ji, the Silver Temple. So he first visited Kinkaku-ji and found that the temple *was covered with *gold. He *was very impressed with the beautiful golden color of the temple.

Next, he took a bus to Ginkaku-ji. He left the bus and started to walk. But he *soon found that he didn't know where he was. Just then, he saw some students and asked them for help. They were junior high school students who came to Kyoto from Chiba on a school trip. One boy said, "We are going to Ginkaku-ji. Why don't you join us?" Tim was very happy to hear that. He talked *a lot with the students. *At last they came to Ginkaku-ji. Tim thanked them for their help. He *was a little surprised to find that the color of the temple was not silver.

> *ALT（外国語指導助手）　on his first visit to Kyoto（彼が初めて京都を訪れる際に）
> Kinkaku-ji, the Golden Temple（金閣寺）　Ginkaku-ji, the Silver Temple（銀閣寺）
> be covered with（〜でおおわれている）　gold（金ぱく）　be impressed with（〜に感動する）
> soon（すぐに）　a lot（たくさん）　at last（ついに）　be surprised（おどろく）

ア　Tim went to Ginkaku-ji before he went to Kinkaku-ji.
イ　Tim met some students on the bus to Ginkaku-ji.
ウ　Tim was surprised to find that Ginkaku-ji was covered with silver.
エ　Tim thanked the students for taking him to Ginkaku-ji.

次のクミ（*Kumi*）とアメリカからの交換留学生（an exchange student）のトム（*Tom*）との会話を読んで，あとの問いに答えなさい。　　　　　　　　　　　　　　〈長崎県改題〉

(On the train)

Tom : Excuse me. Can I sit here?

Kumi : Of course, you can.

Tom : Thank you. I am Tom.

Kumi : I am Kumi. Are you going to Nagasaki?

To 　　　change student and I will go to high school there. The name

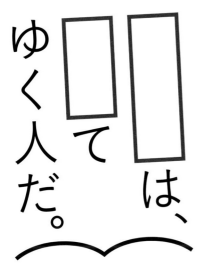

　　　　　　Minato High School.

　　　　　y happy to hear that. I go to the same school. I live near

　　　　　Do you know where you are going to live?

　　　　g to meet my *host family at the station and they will take

　　　　eresting city and many *foreign people visit it. We have

　　　　ivals and nice places to visit. Do you know any famous

　　　　?

　　　　 Park.

　　　　st with my family. We must remember that peace is very

　　　　ant to *pray for peace. I want to do that in the park.

　　　　ve will get to Nagasaki Station soon. I enjoyed talking

　　　　can you take me to some famous places next Sunday?

　　　　 school tomorrow?

　　　　about it then.

ol（ミナト高校）　host family（ホームステイ先の家族）　foreign（外国の）

pray for ～（～を祈る）

　のア～エの中から一つ選びなさい。

　　　and Kumi have been good friends for a long time.

イ　Tom doesn't know where his host family's house is.

ウ　Tom visits Peace Park every summer with his family.

エ　Tom will take Kumi to famous places in Nagasaki.

長文読解（要約文を完成させる）

例題

次の英文は，久美（Kumi）が海外での体験について書いたものです。問いに答えなさい。　　　　　　　　　　　　　　　　　　　〈福島県改題〉

正答率
↓

差がつく!!
A
22%

差がつく!!
B
21%

　　While I was talking with Kate, I *realized something about Kate. She really knew a lot about Australia. She could answer all of my questions. I started to think that I should know more about Japan.

　　We had a great time on our trip. Kate showed us many interesting places, and she taught some useful things. At a *wildlife park, Kate told us to watch the *koalas quietly. She explained, "Koalas usually sleep during the day. If you *make noise, they will wake up. People should enjoy wildlife without *disturbing it. I'll give an example. People may like to hold koalas in their arms, but it *is banned in some areas for wildlife *preservation."

＊realized ～（～に気づいた）　wildlife（野生生物）　koalas（コアラ）　make noise（音を立てる）
disturbing ～（～をじゃますること）　is banned（禁止されている）　preservation（保護）

次の英文は，久美がコアラについて書いたものです。 A と B に入る最も適当な英語を1語ずつ書きなさい。

　　We should remember some things about koalas. At a wildlife park, we should be ┌ A ┐ when we watch them. They sleep during the day. In some areas of Australia, ┌ B ┐ koalas is banned for their preservation. We should enjoy wildlife without disturbing it.

ミスの傾向と対策

　コアラについて書いた文が本文と違った表現になっているので，語の形を変える必要があり，これが正答率が低かった原因かもしれない。まず，コアラについて書いた文の空らんの前後に注目し，どんな品詞の語が入るか考えよう。A は be 動詞のあとなので，名詞か形容詞が，B は □ koalas で主語になるので動名詞が予想できる。

解き方　A　第2段落第3文の「ケイトはコアラを静かに見るように言った」を，「それら（コアラ）を見るときは静かにすべきだ」と表す。副詞 quietly の形容詞 quiet を入れる。
B　最後の文の後半に it is banned「それは禁止されている」とあるが，it は文前半の to hold koalas in their arms「腕にコアラを抱くこと」を指す。1語で表すので to hold を動名詞 holding にする。

解答　A　quiet　　B　holding

入試必出!・要点まとめ

It was **rainy** yesterday. ＝ We had **rain** yesterday.　　「きのうは雨が降りました」
「雨降りの」…形容詞　　　　　　　　　　「雨」…名詞

● 要約文完成のコツ
要約文に適語を補充して完成させる問題は次のような手順で解こう。
① 要約文の空らんの前後に注目し，どんな品詞が入るか推測する。
② 要約文と本文とで共通する表現を手がかりに，本文のどの部分に答えがあるかさがす。
③ 本文と表現が違っている場合は，必要に応じて単語を変えたり，語の形を変えたりする。

1 (35%)　次の英文を読んで，問いに答えなさい。　　　　　　　　　　　　〈埼玉県改題〉

　　Today life in our *society is becoming more and more *convenient. There are some restaurants and stores that are *open twenty-four hours a day. We can use the Internet or send e-mail all day if we want to do so. There are a lot of interesting video games we can play *at any time. In a society like this, our sleeping time is becoming shorter and shorter, and there are a lot of young people who don't go to bed until late at night. They use a lot of time to play video games or send e-mail to their friends. But do you know this life style *may sometimes *cause us some problems?

　　Many people say that having *enough sleep is as important as eating well or *exercising. Our *bodies and brains begin to work when we get up, and they get tired after working for a day. So we need to have enough sleep at night to start another day. What will happen if we don't have enough sleep?

> * society（社会）　convenient（便利な）　open twenty-four hours a day（24時間営業）
> at any time（いつでも）　may ～（～かもしれない）　cause us ～（私たちに～を引き起こす）
> enough（十分な）　exercising（運動すること）　bodies and brains（体と脳）

次の英文は，本文の内容をまとめたものです。次の（　　）にあてはまる英語を，1語書きなさい。

　　In today's very convenient society, there are a lot of young people who don't go to bed until late at night and they sleep only for a short time. This life style may be bad for us and may sometimes cause problems for our bodies and brains. So, like eating well or exercising, it is also（　　）for us to have enough sleep.

2　次の英文を読み，問いに答えなさい。　　　　　　　　　　　　　　　〈福島県改題〉

　　Last December, Kate came to Hiroto's school from *New Zealand. She joined some classes and studied with Hiroto and his *classmates for a week.

　　In the English class on the first day, Kate talked about her family, school and life in New Zealand. Kate also joined the *calligraphy class and wrote easy *kanji*. At lunchtime, Kate showed Hiroto and his friends some pictures. In a picture, Kate had a short *stick in each hand. Hiroto asked her about the picture. Kate answered, "This is a picture my friend took when I practiced the *stick dance at school. Do you know I'm going to do it tomorrow?" "Yes, our teacher told us about that last week. I want to see it," said Hiroto.

（英文は次ページに続く）

The next day, Kate explained about the stick dance. "This is a traditional dance in New Zealand. It's not difficult. Let's dance together." Hiroto and his classmates practiced the dance with Kate. Hiroto could not dance well and sometimes *dropped the sticks. So Kate helped him. Hiroto thought knowing about the *tradition of a foreign country was interesting. He said to Kate, "I'm happy to learn about the stick dance. Do you practice the dance at school?" "Yes," Kate answered. "We usually learn about it at school in New Zealand. I think that's like calligraphy for you, Hiroto." Hiroto found the students in both countries learned about part of their own culture at school.

The last day came. At the *farewell party Hiroto said, "We're going to play the *wadaiko* for you, Kate. Please enjoy our traditional music." Kate said, "I've never listened to the *wadaiko*." Kate was surprised to listen to the *powerful sound. When Hiroto and his friends finished playing the *wadaiko*, Hiroto said to Kate, "Let's play the *wadaiko* together." She said, "I heard you were planning a party to talk together." Hiroto answered, "Yes, but after the dance we changed the plan because we wanted to show you part of our culture in return. So we decided to play the *wadaiko*. We played it at the school festival last month." Kate enjoyed the *wadaiko* and asked Hiroto many questions about it. But Hiroto could not answer well. He thought, "Although I knew a lot about New Zealand, I could not explain about Japan well." Then he noticed. "Communication between people who have different cultures will be more interesting if I can explain more about Japan. It's important to learn about Japanese culture and to tell it to people from foreign countries."

*New Zealand (ニュージーランド)　classmates (同級生)　calligraphy (習字・書写)　stick (棒)
stick dance (スティックダンス〈棒を使った踊り〉)　dropped ～ (～を落とした)　tradition (伝統)
farewell party (さよならパーティー)　powerful (力強い)

次の英文は，Hiroto の考えの変化をまとめたものです。 A と B に入る最も適当な英語を，本文中から A は2語， B は1語でそのまま抜き出して書きなさい。

Hiroto thought it was interesting to know about the culture of a foreign country when he practiced the stick dance. After he played the *wadaiko*, he thought explaining about his own country could make communication with people from foreign countries ☐ A ☐. So he tried to understand more about Japan and to ☐ B ☐ people from foreign countries about its culture.

3 work experience (職場体験) に関する次の英文を読んで，問いに答えなさい。 〈埼玉県改題〉

Yuko is a junior high school student. Last summer all the students in her class had work experience for five days. They worked at libraries, stations, schools, *and so on. Yuko worked at Aoba *Nursery School. She took care of three-year-old children. Before working she thought that the work at a nursery school was just to play with small children and very easy. But after she began to work, she found that she was wrong.

On the first day, Yuko tried to *communicate with the children in the class. She saw a boy reading a picture book. She went to him and said, "Let's read the book together." He looked up at her, but didn't say anything. Soon he looked down and started to read the book again. Then she asked, "What are you reading? Is the book interesting?" He looked up at her again. This time she smiled to him. Suddenly he ran away from her. She was very *shocked. "What did I do? Did I do something bad to him?"

It was time for lunch. The children in the class sat down and began to eat lunch. When they finished eating lunch, Yuko was very shocked to see the room. There was food and milk *everywhere. The children did it because they couldn't eat and drink very well. She had to clean the room. She was very tired.

On the next day, when Yuko was playing with the children in the room, a boy tried to get a book from a girl's hand. The girl *pushed the boy and said, "No. Stop it!" The boy began to cry. Yuko ran to the girl and said, "Don't do that! It is very *dangerous." Then the girl also began to cry. Yuko didn't know what to do.

When Yuko was *in trouble, the teachers at the nursery school always helped her. A teacher said, "Because small children can't communicate well with others like us, teachers have to watch them carefully and try to understand what they are thinking and what they want to do." She also said, "The work at a nursery school is very difficult, but I love this work because the children give me a lot of *energy."

On the last day, when Yuko was cleaning the room, a boy came to her and said, "Please read this book to me, Yuko-*sensei*." She was very happy because he was the boy who ran away from her on the first day. She said to him, "Of course! Let's read together."

When Yuko finished the five days, she felt that working at Aoba Nursery School was really a good *experience for her. The work was very difficult, but the teachers and the children there taught her a lot of things, and they gave her a lot of energy too. Now she is studying very hard to become a nursery school teacher in the future.

> *~ and so on (~など) nursery school (保育園) communicate (気持ちを伝え合う)
> shocked (ショックを受けて) everywhere (いたるところに) pushed ~ (~を押した)
> dangerous (危険な) in trouble (困って) energy (力，エネルギー) experience (経験)

次の英文は，本文の内容をまとめたものです。次の (1) ～ (4) にあてはまる英語を，1 語ずつ書きなさい。

Before working at the nursery school, Yuko thought that (1) with the children was the only work there. But after she began to work at Aoba Nursery School, she found that the work there was very (2) because the teachers had to do a lot of things to take care of the children.

She (3) a lot of things from the work experience there and now her (4) is to become a nursery school teacher.

差がつく!!
1
23%

2
40%

3
28%

4
33%

日本語を英文にする

例題

次の下線部(1)，(2)を英語に直しなさい。　　　〈佐賀県後期〉

正答率
↓

差がつく!!
(1)
20%

差がつく!!
(2)
15%

（電話で）

A：いよいよ明日，日本に帰ってくるのね。

B：短い留学だったわ。(1)もっとこっちにいたいわ。でも，日本も恋しいな。

A：そうでしょうね。(2)帰ったらたくさん話を聞かせてね。

B：うん，いろいろ話したいことがあるわ。

ミスの傾向と対策

(1)「～したい」の表現がわからなかったり，「もっと」を more で表したりといったミスが考えられる。「もっと」はここでは「もっと長く」の意味である。

(2)「帰ったら」や「話を聞かせて」をうまく英語に訳すのが難しかったかもしれない。日本語をそのまま英語に訳そうとせずに，英文にしやすいように日本語を言いかえてみることが大切。

解き方

(1)「～したい」は would like to ～ か want to ～ で表す。「もっと（長く）」は longer で表す。

(2)「帰ったら」は「あなたが帰ったときに」と考えて，when ～ で表す。「たくさん話を聞かせて」は「私にたくさんの話をしてください」と言いかえて，please ～ で表す。「（人）に（もの）を話す」は〈tell ＋人＋もの〉で表せる。

解答　（例）(1) I would like to stay here longer. / I want to be here longer.　(2) When you come back to Japan, please tell me a lot of stories. / Please tell me〔us〕many things about your life there after you come back.

　入試必出! ● **要点まとめ**

I **have been to** Australia before.

have been to ～「～へ行ったことがある」…現在完了

「私は以前オーストラリアへ行ったことがあります」

和文英訳問題では，時制に気をつけて英語に直す必要がある。日本語から判断できないときは，前後の文脈などから判断する。

● **いろいろな時制の文**

①**過去の文**…「～した」

規則動詞…〈原形＋-(e)d〉／不規則動詞…語尾に -(e)d をつけず，それ以外の方法で過去形を作る。

②**未来の文**…「～するだろう，～するつもりだ」

形…〈be going to ＋動詞の原形〉／〈will ＋動詞の原形〉

③**現在完了**…①完了「～したところだ」　②経験「～したことがある」　③継続「（ずっと）～している」

形…〈have〔has〕＋過去分詞〉

1 下線部の日本語を，①は英語8語以内，②は英語10語以内で書きなさい。she's などの短縮形は1語として数え，符号は語数に含めません。　〈長野県改題〉

① 32%
② 28%

　I became interested in *Michael Faraday.　My teacher said, "There is a book which tells us about his last Christmas Lecture."　①私はその本を読んだことがありません。So I would like to read it.　②私は明日図書館に行くつもりです。I want to know about the experiments he did at the lecture.

＊Michael Faraday（マイケル・ファラデー〈19世紀の科学者〉）

2 次の日本語を表す英文を書きなさい。〔4〕は指示に従って書くこと。

差がつく!! 24%　〔1〕たくさんの新しいことをするつもりです。　〈山梨県改題〉

差がつく!! 21%　〔2〕私たちは車で彼らの家に行きました。　〈山梨県改題〉

差がつく!! 19%　〔3〕あなたに私たちのグループに加わってほしい。　〈北海道改題〉

差がつく!! 18%　〔4〕あなたに会えることを楽しみにしています。（looking を使って）　〈宮崎県改題〉

差がつく!! 14%　〔5〕彼は老人たちに彼の考えを話しました。　〈宮城県B改題〉

3 次の下線部〔1〕，〔2〕をそれぞれ英文にしなさい。　〈青森県改題〉

差がつく!! 〔1〕 19%
差がつく!! 〔2〕 11%

　There is a river near my house and my city gets water from it.　〔1〕しかし私は水について知らないことがたくさんあります。For example, how do we get clean water?　〔2〕私は本を読んでそのことについて勉強するつもりです。

4 下線部に英語を書き，（　　）内の場面にふさわしい英文を完成させなさい。英語は6語以上で書きなさい。　〈秋田県〉

17%

A : _____ ?
　　（日本のどういうところが好きか尋ねたいとき）
B : Well, people are very kind.

長文中の空らんを埋める英作文①

例題

正答率
↓
差がつく!!
①②
15%

あなたは父の友人のジム（Jim）さんと話をしています。ジムさんは日本の観光旅行を終えて帰国するところです。対話の流れに合うように（①）と（②）の両方にあなた自身の考えを英語で書きなさい。ただし①②をあわせて20語程度（．，？！などの符号は語数に含まない）とすること。場所や行事名はローマ字で書いてもよい。　　　　　　　　　　　　　　〈千葉県〉

You : Did you have a good time in Japan?

Jim : Yes, I did. I hope I can visit Japan again in the future.

You : Please come and stay with my family next time.

Jim : Thank you. If I come to Japan again, what is the best season to visit?

You : (　　　　　　①　　　　　　)

Jim : Really? Why?

You : (　　　　　　②　　　　　　)

Jim : Oh, I see.

ミスの傾向と対策　　　正答率が低かったのは，空らんに入る文を自分で考えて英語にするのが難しかったからかもしれない。また，①は直前の Jim の the best season to visit の意味がとりづらく，ここを正確に訳すことができないと，空らんに入る文がわかりづらい。②は①の理由を答える文を書くが，自分で自由に発想して，書けそうな文を書くとよい。

解き方　　①　「もしまた日本に来るとしたら，訪れるのに一番いい季節は何ですか」の質問に答える文を書く。自分の考えを述べるので，I think (that) 〜 is the best season.「私は〜が一番いい季節だと思う」の文で表すとよい。
②　①で答えた理由を書く。その季節にできることなどを can「〜できる」を使って表すとよい。

解答　　（例）①　I think that spring is the best season. ②　Because you can see a lot of beautiful flowers and enjoy flower festivals. (21語)

入試必出! ● 要点まとめ

Which season do you like the best? — I like **spring** the best.

「どの季節」→季節を答える
「あなたはどの季節がいちばん好きですか」　　　　　　「私は春がいちばん好きです」
空らんを埋める英作文では，空らんの前後の文脈を把握し，何を答えるべきかを考える必要がある。この例文では Which season「どの季節」と聞かれているので，季節を答えればいいことがわかる。最上級の表現 like 〜 the best を用いて，好きな季節を答える。

● **まず空らんに入る文を推測しよう！**
長文中の空らんを埋める英作文問題では，まず前後の文から会話の流れをつかんで，空らんに入る文を推測しよう。自分の考えを書く場合は，難しい文を書く必要はないので，自分が書けそうな文を考えること。語数などの条件がある場合は，それに合わせて英文を作ろう。

1 次の英文は，カナダ（Canada）人のブラウン先生（Mr. Brown）と，まこと（Makoto）君の対話です。意味が通るように**ア～ウ**に入る英文をそれぞれ１つ書きなさい。　〈青森県改題〉

Makoto : Excuse me, Mr. Brown. Do you have time to talk with me?
Mr. Brown : Sure.
差がつく!! ア 12%
Makoto : I must write a *report in English.　 ア
Mr. Brown : OK. In Canada all teachers have their own classrooms and wait for the students there, but in Japan　 イ
差がつく!! イ 12%
Makoto : I see. *Anything else?
Mr. Brown : Well, schools start in September there, but here in Japan　 ウ
差がつく!! ウ 23%
Makoto : Do students join sports teams?
Mr. Brown : Yes. But they don't have to play the same sport all year. For example, they can join the basketball team in the fall and winter, the *football team in the spring and the soccer team in the summer.

* report（レポート） Anything else?（ほかに何かありますか。） football（アメリカンフットボール）

2 次の〔1〕，〔2〕のそれぞれの対話が成り立つように，下線部に適切な英語を入れなさい。　〈栃木県〉

差がつく!! 20%
〔1〕 *A* : Your guitar is wonderful. Where did you buy it?
　　 B : I don't know, because ＿＿＿＿＿＿＿＿＿. Yesterday was my birthday.
　　 A : Oh! You have a nice father.

差がつく!! 13%
〔2〕 *A* : I'm trying to open this door, but I can't.
　　 B : All right. I think ＿＿＿＿＿＿＿＿＿.
　　 A : Great! Thank you.

3 差がつく!! 19% 次は，亜矢（Aya）の家にホームステイをしていたナンシー（Nancy）に，亜矢が送った手紙と写真です。写真を参考にして，手紙文中の下線部に適切な英語を入れなさい。　〈栃木県改題〉

Dear Nancy,
　Hi, how are you? I am sending you our picture with this letter. Do you remember Takuya's birthday party? I didn't know what to give him. You said, "How about a cake? I ＿＿＿＿＿＿＿＿, so I can help you." Then I made the cake with you. That was the first cake I ever made, and Takuya liked it. In the picture Takuya is smiling between us.
　I really want to see you.

　　　　　　　　　　　　　　　　　Your friend,
　　　　　　　　　　　　　　　　　Aya

長文中の空らんを埋める英作文②

例題

正答率

↓

差がつく!!

11%

あなたは，ホームステイ先で友だちになったポール（Paul）と，スーザン（Susan）のことについて話をしています。対話の流れに合うように（　）にあなた自身の考えを英語で書きなさい。ただし，文の数は2文以上とし，20語程度（. , ? ! などの符号は語数に含まない）とすること。場所の名前や人名などの固有名詞はローマ字で書いてもよい。〈千葉県〉

Paul : Susan will be 15 years old soon. Did you know that?

You : No, I didn't. When is her birthday?

Paul : Next Sunday. Let's do something for her. Do you have any good ideas?

You : Well, how about this? (　　　　　　　　　　　　　　　　　　　)

Paul : That sounds good. She will be happy about that.

ミスの傾向と対策　　正答率が低かったのは，誕生日を祝うアイデアを自分で考えて英語にするのが難しかったからかもしれない。または，アイデアを述べるときにどういう文で表せばよいかが思いつかなかったからかもしれない。まず，書く内容を日本語でまとめてから，英文にしよう。

解き方　　スーザンの誕生日を祝うことになり，ポールの「何かいいアイデアはある？」に答える文を書く。直後のポールの発言を参照し，スーザンが喜ぶような内容の文を書くこと。Let's ～.「～しましょう」などを使って書くとよい。

解答　　（例）Let's buy a present for her and make a birthday cake. We'll also write a beautiful birthday card for her.（2文，20語）

 入試必出! ● **要点まとめ**

How did you go to Hokkaido? — I went there by train.

「どうやって～?」…手段を問う　　　　　　　　　〈by＋乗り物〉…「～で」

「あなたはどうやって北海道へ行きましたか」　「私は列車でそこへ行きました」

● **空らんの前後の文に注目しよう！**

長文中の空らんに適切な文を入れる問題では，前後の文に注目して，文脈に合う文を書かなければならない。決まった受け答えのパターンを覚えておくと書きやすい。

・How long ～?「どれくらい（の間）～?」（期間）— For ～.「～の間です」

・Will〔Can〕you ～?「～してくれませんか」— Sure. / All right.「いいですよ」

・Shall I ～?「（私が）～しましょうか」

　　— Yes, please.「はい，お願いします」/ No, thank you.「いいえ，けっこうです」

1 次の□□□□□は，ある生徒がアリ（ant）の巣の様子を見て1枚の紙にまとめたものです。スケッチとメモをもとにして書いた英文の，[1][2]に適切な英語を入れなさい。　〈栃木県〉

差がつく!! (1) 19%
(2) 38%

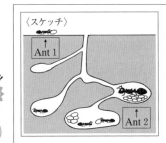

〈メモ〉
○アリは5匹　　○部屋は4つ
○Ant 1・地上に出ている／・食料を運んでいる
○Ant 2・たくさんの卵を持っている／・他よりも大きい
〈英文〉There are five ants. They have made four rooms.
Ant 1 is on the ground. It ___[1]___ to the room.
Ant 2 has many eggs. It ___[2]___ the other ants.

2 次の英文は，オーストラリアの大学内でのトム（Tom）とボブ（Bob）の対話の一部です。意味が通るようにア〜ウに入る英文をそれぞれ1つ書きなさい。　〈青森県改題〉

ア 32%
イ 35%
差がつく!! ウ 23%

Tom : How was your vacation in Japan?
Bob : It was great. I had a good time.
Tom : Good. | ア |
Bob : I stayed for three weeks.
Tom : | イ |
Bob : Well, I enjoyed *snowboarding and visiting *hot springs. I saw a snow festival too.
Tom : A snow festival?
Bob : Yes. In the festival people can see many big snow *statues in a park. At night they are *illuminated and they are beautiful.
Tom : That sounds wonderful, but very cold too.

Bob : Don't worry. When you feel cold, you can eat something hot. *Noodles in hot soup helped me to stay warm.
Tom : I see. I don't like winter. But I think the festival makes winter there exciting.
Bob : Yes. I hope you will enjoy winter there in the future. At my house I can show you the video I took. | ウ |
Tom : Yes, I'd like to.

* snowboarding（スノーボードをすること）
hot springs（温泉） statues（像）
illuminated（ライトで照らされて）
noodles in hot soup（温かいスープに入った麺）

自由英作文（絵・資料を使った問題）

AからDへと場面が連続する4枚の絵があります。この一連の絵の内容を，5文以上の英語で，読む人にわかりやすく伝えられるよう工夫して書き表しなさい。

〈岐阜県〉

正答率
↓
47%

ミスの傾向と対策

正答率が低かったのは，自分でストーリーを考えて英文にするのが難しかったからかもしれない。この問題では，「寝坊してあわてて学校に行ったら土曜日だった」というストーリーを順序よく5文以上でまとめる必要がある。また，動詞の過去形を正しく書けなかったといったミスも考えられる。まず絵を見て日本語でストーリーを組み立てて，自分が書けそうな英文で表現しよう。

解き方
A「少年が起きたら8時だった」B「走って学校へ行った」C「校門が閉まっていた」D「土曜日で学校は休みだと気がついた」get up「起きる」，hurry to ～「急いで～へ行く」，realize that ～「～と気づく」などの表現が使える。

解答
（例）The boy usually gets up at seven, but that morning he got up at eight. School starts at 8:20, so he hurried to school. When he got to school, the gate was closed. Just then he realized that it was Saturday. There was no school that day.（5文）

 入試必出！ 要点まとめ

It **was** sunny last Sunday. So I **went** to the park to play tennis with my
　　isの過去形　　　　　　　　　　　　　　goの過去形
sister. We **enjoyed** playing it very much.
　　　　　　　enjoyの過去形
「この前の日曜日は晴れていました。それで私は姉（妹）とテニスをしに公園に行きました。私たちはそれをするのをとても楽しみました」
長めの自由英作文では，全体としてまとまりがあるかに注意し，適切な接続詞を用いて文をつなげるようにする。また，時制を統一する必要がある場合は，動詞にも注意しよう。

● **絵や資料からわかることをつかんでから英文を作る。**
　絵や資料を使った自由英作文は，まずそれらからわかることをつかんでから，日本語で内容をまとめ，英文にしよう。ストーリーのある絵の場合は，絵の中の人物の行動や表情に注目し，ストーリーを組み立てていこう。

1 41% AからDへと場面が連続する4枚の絵があります。この一連の絵の内容を，5文以上の英語で，読む人にわかりやすく伝えられるよう工夫して書き表しなさい。　〈岐阜県後期〉

2 差がつく!! 24% あなたは英語の授業で，Computers in our life というテーマの発表をすることになりました。あなたが発表する内容を，4文以内の英文で書きなさい。なお，必要があれば次の資料を参考にしてもかまいません。　〈新潟県改題〉

中学生のパソコンの使用目的（複数回答）

	Boys	Girls
To use the Internet	75.0%	68.0%
To play games	64.3%	53.2%
To *exchange e-mails	15.3%	25.4%
To listen to music	12.3%	14.3%
*Others	12.0%	14.7%

* exchange（交換する）　others（その他）

3 差がつく!! 16% 映画館の入口で2人の女の子が会話をしています。この映画館には四つの部屋があり，2人はそれぞれの部屋で上映される映画のタイトルと開始時刻を見ながら話をしています。1〜4の会話の流れに合うように，絵の中の（　　）に入る英文を4語以上の1文で書きなさい。　〈長崎県A改題〉

自由英作文（手紙文を書く）

例題

次は，カナダに住む友達のエレン（Ellen）から送られてきた電子メールの最後の部分です。あなたなら，エレンへどのような返事を書きますか。A には 4 語以上，B には 5 語以上の英語で書きなさい。　　　〈福島県〉

正答率

↓

35%

エレンからの電子メール	エレンへの電子メール
This year, I'm going to study Japanese to visit you in Japan. What are you going to do this year? I hope to hear from you soon. Ellen	Hi, Ellen. Wishing you all the best in 2022. Thank you for your e-mail. I'm sending this to answer your question. I'm going to ⬚ A ⬚ because ⬚ B ⬚ .

ミスの傾向と対策

　　文の一部を英語で書く問題だが，正答率は低かった。be going to のあとに動詞の原形が書けていない，because のあとに理由を表す文が書けていないといったミスが考えられる。難しい文を書く必要はないので，前後をよく見て，文脈に合った文を書くようにしよう。

解き方　　「あなたは今年何をするつもりですか」に答える文を書く。「私は ⬚ B ⬚ だから ⬚ A ⬚ するつもりです」という文を完成させる。A は I'm going to のあとなので動詞の原形で始まる語句を書く。B には A の理由を書く。

解答　　（例）(I'm going to) _A practice baseball hard with my friends (because) _B I want to come in first in the city tournament(.) (A：6 語，B：10 語)

 入試必出！ 要点まとめ

Thank you for your letter. You told me about your summer vacation.
Thank you for ～.「～をありがとう」
I'm going to visit Okinawa with my family.
　be going to ～「～するつもりだ」
「お手紙ありがとう。あなたはあなたの夏休みについて私に話してくれました。私は私の家族と沖縄を訪れるつもりです」

● **相手にお礼や予定などを伝える。**
　手紙文を書く問題では，いろいろな設定が出題されるので，答える内容もさまざまだ。多く出されるのが，相手の手紙を読んで，文中の質問に答える返事を書く，という設定だ。相手が知りたいことは何かをしっかりつかんで書くようにしよう。また，お礼の手紙を出す，という設定では，感謝の気持ちが十分伝わるような文面にしよう。

1 (44%)

あなたは，次の〔　　〕内のいずれか1つを誕生日のプレゼントとしてもらいました。

〔bag　bike　book　cake　CD player〕

下の①，②の条件にしたがって，お礼の手紙を完成させなさい。

①あなたがもらったプレゼントを "Thank you very much for the ＿＿." の ＿＿ に書くこと。

②前後の英語とつながるように，お礼の手紙の ＿＿ に入る30語程度の英語を考え，書くこと。ただし，コンマやピリオドなどの記号は語数に含めないこと。　　　　〈大阪府共通〉

お礼の手紙

> Dear △△△,
>
>   Thank you very much for the ＿＿＿＿.
>
>
>
>   Thank you again.　I'd like to see you soon.
>
>   Yours,
>
>   ○○○

2

Yuko は，昨年マサチューセッツ州のボストンに帰った ALT の Richard 先生に，はがきを書くことになりました。次にあげるのは，Yuko の書いたはがきです。このはがきを見て，下の(1)(2)の問いに答えなさい。　　　　〈高知県〉

>   March 11, 20XX
>
> Dear Mr. Richard Smith,
>
>   How are you?　It's cold in Kochi.
>
>   I'm going to Boston on March 25th.
>
>   &boxed{A}　I'm *looking forward to this trip.
>
>   I want to talk to you again.　&boxed{B}
>
> After that, please show me around your town.
>
>   With love,
>
>   Yuko
>
>
>
> NIPPON 70
>
> Mr. Richard Smith
>
> ○○○○○○
>
> Boston, Massachusetts
>
> U.S.A.

* look forward to ～（～を楽しみにする）

(差がつく!!) (12%) (1) &boxed{A} に，アメリカに行くのが初めてであることを伝える英語1文を書きなさい。

(差がつく!!) (12%) (2) &boxed{B} に，昼食をいっしょに食べることを誘う英語1文を書きなさい。

自由英作文（自己紹介・説明）

あなたが高校に入学後，取り組んでみたいことを1つ取り上げ，そのことについて次の条件に従って書きなさい。 〈秋田県〉

条件：内容につながりのある英文を3文以上書くこと。

ミスの傾向と対策　内容につながりのある英文を3文以上書かなければならないので難しく，正答率も低かった。自由英作文は，まとまりのある文を書いたり，テーマに沿った適切な表現を使うことが難しい。まず日本語で内容を整理してから，自分が書けそうな英文で書くようにしよう。また，過去数年の入試に目を通し，よく出題されるテーマの問題に取り組むことで，英文で記述する力を磨いておくとよい。

解き方　自分が好きなものや興味のあるものを取り上げ，高校生活に向けての意欲を具体的に書く。I'd like to〔I want to〕～.「～したい」などの文を使うとよい。解答例は「私は理科が好きなので，理科クラブの部員になりたいです。私は多くの種類の鳥に興味があります。それらについてもっと勉強したいと思います」という意味。

解答　（例）I like science, so I'd like to be a member of the science club. I'm interested in many kinds of birds. I want to study more about them.（3文）

 **入試必出！ 要点まとめ**

My hobby is swimming. **I think** swimming is good for my health.
「私は～と思う」

I'd like to visit Australia and enjoy swimming there.
I'd like to ～「私は～したい」

「私の趣味は水泳です。水泳は私の健康にいいと思います。私はオーストラリアを訪れて，そこで水泳を楽しみたいです」

● **自己紹介や説明する文でよく使われる表現**

　・This is ～.「これは～です」

　・My hobby is ～.「私の趣味は～です」

　・I like ～.「私は～が好きです」

　・I want to ～. / I'd like to ～.「私は～したいです」

　・～ because … .「…だから～」（理由を述べる）

　・I think〔thought〕～.「私は～と思います〔思いました〕」

1 あなたの宝物（大切にしているもの）について，次の一連の質問に対する答えを英語で書きなさい。ただし，(1)は5語以上の1文，(2)は8語以上の1文で書くこと。（「,」「.」などの符号は語として数えない。）　　　　　　〈愛媛県〉

39% (1) あなたの宝物は何ですか。

差がつく!! **20%** (2) また，どうしてそれがあなたの宝物なのですか。

2 **30%** 次の英文中の下線部の問いに対して，あなたならどのように答えるか。下の□□の中の形式に従って英語で書きなさい。　　　　　　　　〈佐賀県後期〉

　　You got an e-mail from your friend in London.　She wants to visit your *hometown this year.　What do you want to show her?

　　　　　　　　　* hometown（生まれ故郷，または現在住んでいる町，市，県など）

I want to show her (　　　) because (　　　　　　　　　　　　　　　).

3 「中学校時代の思い出」というテーマで英語の学校新聞を作ることになりました。中学校時代の思い出としてあなた自身の心に残っていることについて，次の一連の質問に対する答えを英語で書きなさい。ただし，(1)は8語以上の1文，(2)は5語以上の1文で書くこと。（「,」「.」などの符号は語として数えない。）　　　　　　〈愛媛県〉

27% (1) あなたはどのようなことをしましたか。

差がつく!! **22%** (2) また，あなたはそれについてどう思いましたか。

4 差がつく!! **18%** your hobby（あなたの趣味）について，あなたはどんなスピーチをするか。次の条件に従って書きなさい。　　　　　　〈秋田県〉

条件：内容につながりのある英文を3文以上書くこと。

5 差がつく!! **11%** 次のように問われたとき，あなたならどのような speech をするか。5つの英文で書きなさい。　　　　　　〈山梨県〉

　　Will you make a speech in English to introduce Japan?　(Please choose something to talk about like beautiful places in Japan, Japanese festivals, Japanese food, or our school life.)

 重要な単語・熟語

解答　本冊 P.9

1 second
2 (e)asy
3 (l)ook
4 (1)runner　(2)taking

解説

1 On the ☐ day of the trip を「旅行の二日目に」という意味にするためには，空らんに「何番目の」を表す序数を入れる。「2番目の」はsecond。

2 「私は日本語の本を読んでいるの。それは私には難しすぎる。どうか私を助けて！　もしこのメールを読んだら，私に電話してね」より，「キャシーはその日本語の本は彼女にとって簡単ではないと思っている」という文にする。「簡単な」はeasy。

3 迷子犬についての英文。「グリーンさんは人々に，彼の犬をさがすよう頼んでいる」という文にする。「～をさがす」はlook for ～。

4 (1)A「電車に遅れそうよ。急いで！　走って，ジェームズ。もっと速く走って！」B「できないよ。私はきみのように若くないんだ。けれども私は若いときには，速いランナー（走る人）だったよ」
(2)A「ユキコ，これは私のイヌの写真よ」B「わあ，あなたのイヌはとてもかわいいわね！　このイヌはアメリカにいるの？」A「ええ。私の家族が，私のかわりに彼を世話しているの。本当に彼に会いたいわ」 take care of ～「～の世話をする」 空らんの前にbe動詞があるので，現在進行形にすることに注意。

一般動詞（現在形・過去形）

解答　本冊 P.11

1 wrote　**2** taught
3 （例）I went to bed at ten.
4 （例）What did you write
5 （例）I told him about my school life in English.

解説

1 空らんの前の2文は「彼は伝統的な日本文化に興味があると言いました。それで，私は彼に和紙のはがきの1枚を送ることに決めました」という意味。空らんを含む文は「その晩，私はそれに英語で彼へのメッセージを☐，そして翌朝それを彼に送りました」なので，はがきにメッセージを「書いた」という意味になるように，write「～を書く」を選び，過去形wroteにして入れる。

2 last year「昨年」があるので，過去形taughtにする。「だれが昨年あなた（たち）に英語を教えましたか」という文になる。

3 「あなたは昨夜何時に寝ましたか」という過去の疑問文。動詞goを過去形wentにして「私は～時に寝ました」と答える。「～時に」は〈at＋時刻〉で表す。

4 エミは「昨日アメリカの友達に手紙を書きました」と言い，「私は自分の夢について書きました」と答えているから，「あなたは手紙に何について書きましたか」と尋ねる文にする。一般動詞の過去の疑問文はdidを使い，動詞は原形write。

5 「～に…について話す」はtell ～ about …。tellの過去形はtold。「英語で」はin English。

現在完了

本冊 P. 13

解答

1 (1)heard　(2)done　(3)playing

2 イ

3 (1)have not had a chance
(2)have never read them to the children
(3)have been waiting for him since

4 (例) I've〔I have〕 never heard of〔about〕 it〔that〕.

解説

1 (1)直前にhaveがあるので，現在完了になるように，過去分詞にする。hearの過去分詞はheard。
(2)前にI've（＝I have）alreadyがあるので，現在完了になるように，過去分詞にする。doの過去分詞はdone。
(3)直前にbe動詞の過去分詞beenがあるので，現在完了進行形の疑問文になるように，動詞のing形にする。A「彼女はどれぐらいの間ピアノを弾いているのですか」B「2時間です」

2 あとのthen「そのとき」より，「そのとき以来」の意味になるイのsinceが適切。「私はそのとき以来，たくさんのおもしろいことを見つけてきました」 現在完了ではforとsinceの使い分けを押さえることが重要。

3 語群のhaveや過去分詞に着目して，現在完了の文を組み立てる。(1)have a chance to ～で「～する機会がある」。現在完了のhaveと，一般動詞haveの過去分詞hadを混同しないよう注意。「でも，私は日本に来て以来，それ（＝ピアノ）を弾く機会がありません」 (2)readは過去分詞もread。neverがあるのでhave never read「読んだことがない」という文にする。「しかし，私たちはそれら（＝英語で書かれた，人気の日本の物語）を子どもたちに読んだことがありません」 (3)beenとwaitingから，現在完了進行形の文にする。forはwait for ～「～を待つ」で使う。sinceとforの使い分けに注意。「私たちは朝からずっと彼を待っ

ています。しかし彼はまだここにいません」

4 「初耳だよ」は「聞いたことがない」と考え，neverを用いた現在完了の否定文で表す。

 不定詞

本冊 P. 15

解答

1 (1)イ→エ→ア→ウ　(2)エ→ア→ウ→イ

2 It was a lot of fun to play

3 (1)told you to finish it
(2)it will be fun to visit museums
(3)do you have anything to

4 (1)イ→エ→ウ
(2)イ→ア→エ

解説

1 (1)decide to ～で「～することを決める，～する決心をする」。「ソフィーは外国に行く決心をした」 (2)letに着目。〈let＋目的語＋動詞の原形〉で「～に…させてやる」。let me knowは直訳すると「私に知らせてください」だが，「私に教えてください」と訳すと自然な日本語になる。「私にあなたのアイデアを教えてください」

2 〈it is ～ to＋動詞の原形〉「…することは～だ」の形を使う。ここは過去の文。〈～〉にはa lot of funを，動詞の原形にはplayを置く。

3 (1)〈tell ～ to＋動詞の原形〉で「～に…するように言う」を表す。
(2)〈it is ～ to＋動詞の原形〉「…することは～だ」の文。isを推量のwill beにする。
(3)まずdo you have anythingと続け，anythingを修飾する形容詞的用法の不定詞to eatをあとに続ける。

4 (1)〈want ～ to＋動詞の原形〉を用いて，〈～〉にeveryone，動詞の原形にseeを置き，「私はみんなにそれを見てほしいです」とする。
(2)helpに続くのはhimかthem。Aの発言より，手伝おうとしている相手はTomなのでhelp himが適切。動詞の原形carryがあるの

で，〈help＋目的語＋動詞の原形〉「〜が…するのを手伝う」を用いて help him carry them「彼がそれらを運ぶのを手伝う」とする。

 分詞

本 冊 P. 17

解答

1 a wonderful book written by an American woman
2 students wearing uniforms in
3 (1) look at the pictures taken during your trip
　(2) half of the people working in
4 エ
5 they books written for children

解説

1 まず It is a wonderful book「それはすばらしい本です」を作る。「アメリカの女性によって書かれた」は written by an American woman で表し，book のあとに置く。

2 the students のあとに wearing uniforms を続けると，「制服を着ている生徒」という意味になる。

3 (1) look at the pictures とし，「あなたの旅行中に撮られた写真」となるように，taken during your trip を pictures に続ける。
　(2) 直前の文から，スーパーマーケットで働く人々の話題だとわかる。文頭の About に half of the people を続け，どのような人々なのかを後ろから現在分詞 working 〜で修飾する形にする。「このスーパーマーケットで働いている人々の約半分ほどが，50歳を超えています」

4 「約400年前に建てられたお寺」と考えると自然なので，「建てられた」という受け身の意味を表す過去分詞の**エ** built を選ぶ。

5 Are they books? という疑問文を作り，written for children を books の後に置くと「子どものために書かれた本」という意味になる。

 関係代名詞

本 冊 P. 19

解答

1 pictures he sent to
2 (1) me to speak about a lot of things I learned
　(2) drivers read the words you wrote
　(3) of the books I found showed
3 （例）I helped a woman who〔that〕spoke〔talked〕to me in English.

解説

1 some に続けられるのは pictures。これを he sent to us が後ろから修飾する形にする。he の前に目的格の関係代名詞が省略されていると考える。

2 (1)〈tell 〜 to＋動詞の原形〉で「〜に…するように言う」を表すので，(told) me to speak about a lot of things と続ける。さらに a lot of things を I learned in Japan が後ろから修飾する形にする。I の前に目的格の関係代名詞が省略されていると考える。
　(2) can で始まる疑問文なので，あとに〈主語＋動詞の原形〉が続く。動詞の原形は read を使う。「車を運転する人は〜を読めますか」という内容になると考えられるので，can drivers read the words と the words を you wrote が後ろから修飾する形にする。you の前に目的格の関係代名詞が省略されていると考える。
　(3)〈one of＋複数形の名詞〉で「〜のうちの1つ」を表すので，One of the books とつなげる。found と showed どちらが文全体の動詞になるかを考える。「私が見つけた本の1つには，〜とあった」という内容になるように，the books を I found が後ろから修飾する形にする。ここまでを文の主語とすると，文全体の動詞は showed にすればよいことがわかる。

3 まず「私は女性を助けました」という文を作り，どのような女性か関係代名詞を用いて説明を加える英文にするとよい。「話しかけてきた」と

過去形なので，関係代名詞のあとの動詞も過去形にする。「英語で」はin English。

 ## そのほかの重要文法①
（比較・動名詞・受動態）

解答 本冊 P. 21

1 (1)not run as fast as
　　(2)picture on your right was painted
2 (1)イ　(2)エ
3 (1)were enjoying talking in a soft
　　(2)nothing is more important than spending time with
　　(3)was the most difficult wall to
4 is used to carry many kinds of things

解説

1 (1)否定文Hideki does not runをまず作り，〈not as ～ as …〉で「…ほど～ない」という意味を表すので，as fast as Ichiroと続ける。(2)The picture was painted by ～.という受動態の文にする。on your right「あなたの右側にある」はThe pictureのあとに置く。

2 (1)前にis notがあるので，動詞のing形にして現在進行形の文にするか，過去分詞にして受動態の文にするかのどちらか。「その化学薬品は売られていない」と受動態の文にするのが適切。sellの過去分詞のイ soldを選ぶ。(2)前置詞aboutの後なのでing形にする。How about ～ing?「～するのはどうですか」

3 (1)〈enjoy ～ing〉で「～して楽しむ」という意味。in a soft voice「静かな声で」
(2)語群のnothing，more，thanなどより，〈nothing is ＋比較級 than …〉「…より～なものはない」という文になると考えられる。「子どもと時を過ごすことほど大切なことはない」spend time「時を過ごす」
(3)It was the wall.という文のwallの前に最上級the most difficultを置き，to breakをwallのあとに置くと，「それは破るのが最も難しい壁だった」という意味になる。

4 「それは使われます」はIt is usedとする。「～を運ぶのに」はto carry ～で表し，「さまざまなもの」はmany kinds of thingsとすればよい。

 ## そのほかの重要文法②
（間接疑問・疑問詞＋to do）

解答 本冊 P. 23

1 ア
2 (1)エ→イ→ウ→オ→ア
　　(2)オ→ウ→イ→ア→エ
3 (1)imagine what our lives will be
　　(2)know what time it is
　　(3)showed us how to grow

解説

1 （　）以降が間接疑問の文。hard「一生懸命に」の前に置けるのはアのhowのみ。「あなたのお母さんは，あなたがどんなに一生懸命バレーボールを練習しているか知っていました」という意味になる。

2 (1)疑問文なので，ウのhow muchかエのdo youで文を始める。How much is this *tenugui*?とすると語句が余るので，Do you knowで始め，間接疑問を続ける。「あなたはこの手ぬぐいがいくらか知っていますか」this *tenugui* isの語順に注意。(2)canの疑問文。Can youに動詞の原形decideが続く。さらにwhich sweet「どの菓子」に〈to＋動詞の原形〉を続けると過不足なく語句を使える。「あなたはどのお菓子を買うべきか決められますか」

3 (1)will，what，be，（　）のあとのlikeに着目。What is ～ like?「～はどんなものですか」の未来形What will ～ be like?「～はどんなものになりますか」を，I can't imagineに間接疑問として続けると，what ～ will be likeという語順になる。〈～〉に入る間接疑問の主語はour lives。「私たちがもっと年をとったとき，私たちの生活がどのようになるか，想像できません」 (2)時間を尋ねる疑問文にする。

「今何時かわかりますか」 what time it isの語順に注意。(3) how to grow 〜「〜の育て方」〈疑問詞＋to do〉が，SVOOの2つ目の目的語になっている文。「そこでは，祖父が私たちにコメの育て方を見せてくれました」

仮定法

本冊 P. 25

解答

1 (1)there were an amusement park in
(2)If I knew her phone number
(3)I wish I could help you

2 （例）he were here now / I could see him every day / I lived in America

3 （例）私がもっと料理が得意だったらなあ。

4 (1)（例）If I were you, I wouldn't buy the 〔that〕 book.
(2)（例）I wish my house were larger 〔bigger〕.

5 （例）I would watch more movies. / I would travel around Japan.

解説

1 (1)まずan amusement parkをまとめ，文末にin my townと続ける。残ったwould，there，wereのうち，つなげて文にできるのはthere were。wouldが不要。「私の町に遊園地があったらなあ」 (2)文の後半より，If 〜の仮定法の文になると考えられる。主語と動詞の過去形，目的語になるものをまとめると，不要な語は現在形のknow。「もし彼女の電話番号を知っていたら，今すぐ彼女に電話できるのに」 (3)語群より，主語はIかyou，（助）動詞はcould，help，wishのいずれかとなる。If I 〜やIf you 〜で始めると語句が余り文を組み立てられない。ここはI wish 〜の形を使い，「私があなたを手伝えたらいいのですが，今は時間がありません」という文にする。ifが不要。

2 アメリカに行った友人に会いたいという会話。「彼がここにいればいいのに」「彼に毎日会えればいいのに」「私がアメリカに住んでいればいい

のに」など，実現する可能性がほとんどない願望を表す文にする。

3 be good at 〜ing「〜するのが得意〔上手〕である」が比較級になっていることに注意。

4 (1)「もし私があなたなら」はIf I were you。後半の「〜しないでしょう」は仮定法の形で，I would not 〜とする。
(2)「〜ならなあ」という願望は仮定法のI wish 〜を使って表す。「もっと広い」は比較級のlarger〔bigger〕を使う。

5 「もしもっとたくさんの自由時間があったら，何をしますか」という問い。現実とは異なることについて述べるので，I would 〜.で答える。解答例は「もっとたくさん映画を見るでしょう」「日本中を旅するでしょう」。このように仮定法を使った英作文が出題されることもあるので，ふだんから自分の答えを準備しておこう。

長文読解
（適切な語句を選ぶ）

本冊 P. 27

解答

1 エ **2** ①ウ ②イ ③カ
3 Ⓐウ Ⓑエ **4** asked

解説

1 Give me juice.「ジュースをちょうだい」をていねいな言い方にかえるので，「ジュースをもらえますか」という文にする。エMay Iが適切。

（要約）
オーストラリアでホームステイをした有紀は，「こんにちは」と「ありがとう」と言うことが，意思疎通によいということを学ぶ。グリーン先生は，アメリカで両親が「お願いします」と「ありがとう」をほかの人に言うようにいつも言っていたことを話す。また，日本語のあいさつがとても好きだと話す。

2 ①「この短い物語を読んだあとで」とする。after 〜ingで「〜したあとで」。
②③どちらもso 〜 that …「とても〜なので…」の構文中にある。どちらにも動詞（didと

meant）の目的語が入るので，somethingか
nothing。「クリキンディはとてもささいなこ
とをしたので，ほかの者は彼の行動は意味がな
い〔何も意味しない〕と思った」となるよう，
②にsomething，③にnothingを入れる。

（要約）
　クリキンディという名前のハチドリの短い物語
を紹介したい。ある日森で火事があり，ほかの
動物はすべて逃げたのに，クリキンディは森に
とどまり，火を消そうとした。クリキンディ
は，自分にできることをしたまでだが，ほかの
動物は，クリキンディがしたことはとてもささ
いであったため意味がないと思った。みなさん
はクリキンディについてどう考えるだろうか。

3 Ⓐは，どの選択肢を入れても文法的には正しい
　文になるため，文脈に合う正しい語を選ぶ。前
　にbe動詞wereがあり，選択肢はすべて過去
　分詞として用いられるので受け身の文になる。
　「多くのボランティアがその催しのために必要
　とされた」となるよう，neededを選ぶ。Ⓑは，
　stopsが動詞と気づかず，bus stopsを「バス
　停」ととらえてしまうと動詞のない文となり，
　意味がとれなくなるので注意する。「どのバス
　が競技場で止まりますか」となるよう，Which
　を選ぶ。

（要約）
　私の市でバレーボールワールドカップ大会が開
催され，多くのボランティアが必要とされた。
私の姉は，駅で英語が話せるガイドとして，外
国人を助けるために働いた。ある日，姉に会い
に駅に行った私は，外国人にどのバスに乗れば
よいかと聞かれ，英語で答えることができた。
私は，それをいい経験だと思い，その日以来，
より一生懸命英語を勉強している。

4 直前の「あなたたちはどうやって卒業記念アル
　バム用の写真を手に入れたのですか」に答える
　文。あとに〈to＋動詞の原形〉の形のto bring
　があることに注目する。「私たちは友達や先生
　方に学校の行事の写真を持ってくるように頼み
　ました」とする。〈ask＋人＋to＋動詞の原形〉
　で「（人）に～するように頼む」の意味。

（要約）
　早紀は友達と卒業記念アルバムを作り終えた。
ラッド先生は早紀にアルバム用の写真をどう
やって手に入れたかといった質問をして，早紀
はそれらに答える。また，卒業記念の活動とし
て，さらに今，早紀たちはビデオも作っている
ことを話す。早紀は，そのビデオは卒業式の前
日に3年生で見ることになっており，ラッド先
生もそれに映っていると話す。

長文読解
（適切な文を選ぶ）

本冊
P. 31

解答
　ウ

解説

　テッドがアメリカの自分の学校と日本の学校の
違いを述べている場面。テッドの「例えば，違
いの1つは教室での昼食だ」に対する康平の言
葉を考える。このあとテッドは「アメリカのぼ
くの学校では，生徒は家から持ってきたお弁当
を食べに学校内の生徒用の食堂へ行く。その食
堂で昼食を買うこともできる」と，違いを説明
しているので，康平は**ウ**の「どういう意味？」
と尋ねたと考えられる。

（要約）
　康平はテッドの兄〔弟〕が9月に高校に入学する
と聞き，アメリカでは学校はたいてい9月に始
まり6月に終わることを知る。さらに康平は，ア
メリカの学校では昼食を教室ではなく学校内の
生徒用の食堂で食べることも知る。また，康平
はアメリカのほとんどの学校には制服がないこ
とを知っていたが，それをテッドに確かめる。

長文読解
（適切な語を書く）

本冊
P. 33

解答
1 to
2 Why are you
3 （例）talk with

1 took meのあとに場所を表す語句があるので，「私をハンバーガーショップへ連れていった」となるよう，toを入れる。〈take＋人＋to 〜〉で「(人)を〜へ連れていく」という意味になる。

（要約）

【ホワイト先生のスピーチ】日本に来て興味深く感じた例として，便利な日本語の「どうも」や，いろいろな種類の自動販売機がありコンビニも多いので，簡単に必要なものが買えること，写真でのピースサインを挙げる。

【健二のスピーチ】アメリカで興味深かったのは，アメリカ人が話す英語がとても速かったこと，すべてが大きかったこと，食事をいつ食べ始めて，いつ終えればよいのかわからなかったことだった。

2 〈Because＋現在の文.〉が答えであること，直後にtakingがあることから，whyで始まる現在進行形の疑問文にする。第1段落第4文のI didn't see why he was doing that「私はなぜ彼がそれをしている（＝盆栽の写真を撮っている）のかわからなかった」より「あなたはなぜそれの写真を撮っているのですか」と問う文にする。Whyのあとに〈be動詞＋主語＋〜ing ...?〉を続ける。Because 〜. の答えから疑問詞whyを使った疑問文にするのはわかりやすいが，補充する語が3語と多いことや，答えの文が問いと同じ現在進行形でないことに注意。疑問詞のあとの語順や，現在進行形のbe動詞を間違えないようにする。前後の文に注目して，適切な疑問詞や文の形を考えよう。

（要約）

よしこは，父の友人であるブラウンさんが，よしこの家で盆栽の写真を撮っているのを不思議に思った。理由を尋ねたところ，盆栽はすばらしいので，アメリカの友人に写真を送りたいからだとブラウンさんは答えた。よしこは，ブラウンさんが，日本についてたくさんのことを知っていることに驚き，日本には，自分が気づかなかった良いものがあるのだと思う。よしこは，外国の人たちとの会話を通して，もっと日

本について学びたいと思っている。

3 由実とジェーンが修学旅行の2日目の午後の予定を計画している場面。ジェーンが大学で日本文学の講義を聞く案を思いつき，由実も「それはいい考えね」と言っている。このあとに続く「明日私たちの計画についてほかのメンバー〜しましょう」という文を完成させる。空らんには「〜と話す」talk withなどが考えられる。

（要約）

由実とジェーンは，修学旅行の2日目のグループの予定を立てている。由実は自分で立てた午前中の予定をジェーンに見せ，ジェーンは，彼女たちのグループのメンバーは物語を書くことに興味がある，と言って文学館に行く案に賛成する。由実は午後どこを訪れたらよいかジェーンに尋ねる。ジェーンは大学で日本文学の講義を受ける案を思いつき，2人は明日ほかのメンバーと話すことにした。由実は，修学旅行は将来について考えるいい機会になると思っている。

長文読解（本文の内容に合う文を完成させる）

本冊 P. 37

解答

1 ウ **2** エ **3** エ
4 エ **5** ア

解説

1 「料理長はけんじに料理長のやり方で料理するように言った，なぜなら」に続く文。第8段落後半に「私はここのすべての料理人によい料理人になってほしい。あなたはまず私のやり方で料理の仕方を学ばなければならない」とあるので，ウの「彼（料理長）は彼（けんじ）に料理が上手になってほしかった」が適切。

（要約）

私の生徒だったけんじはある日，料理学校の体験入学に行ってみた。その学校の生徒と料理を楽しんだ彼は，料理人になる決心をした。高校卒業後に彼はその料理学校へ行き，必死で勉強した。卒業後，彼はこの市の和食レストランで

働き始めた。2年目のある日，料理長はけんじに昼食を作らせたが，それを食べなかった。料理長のやり方で作らなかったからだ。けんじは困難を乗り越えてよい料理人になった。

2 設問文と共通する表現が第2段落冒頭にあるので，該当箇所は見つけやすいが，答えとなる部分が選択肢では言いかえられていることに注意。「カズコが小学生のとき」に続く文を選ぶ。第2段落に小学生のときのことが書かれている。第2文に，英会話学校へ通っていた理由として，I was interested in American movies and going to America「アメリカの映画とアメリカへ行くことに興味があった」とあるので，**エ**の「彼女はアメリカを訪れることを考えていた」が適切。

（要約）
私は幼いころ，内気で，頼まなくても周りの人が何でもしてくれたので，自分の気持ちを表現する必要がなかった。小学生のときには，音楽が好きで，毎日ピアノの練習をした。毎週英会話の学校にも行っていた。

3 「ダイアナは〜がわかった」という文。第5段落まではダイアナが日本でいろいろ体験したことが書かれている。第6段落にそれらを総括したダイアナの感想が書かれているので，この段落に注目する。第7文にBut there are some things 〜.「でもある国を訪れるまで，その国についてわからないことがある」とあるので，これと同じ**エ**が適切。

（要約）
この前の夏，オーストラリアから来た学生のダイアナが東京のホテルに泊まったあと，私の家にホームステイした。彼女は滞在中にいろいろなことを学んだ。日本のホテルや病院には4で終わる部屋番号がない場合もあることや，日本人のふだんの「緑茶」の飲み方，夏祭りに着る浴衣など。ダイアナは，実際にその国に来るまで，わからないことがあると学んだ。

4 設問のJenny's father ran to the phoneという表現は英文中に見つけることができるが，

答えの該当部分は直接的な表現ではなく，そのような行動に出た理由を，話の流れから読みとる必要がある。長文を読むときは，つねに文脈をつかみながら読み進めるようにしよう。
解答は「ジェニーの父親は電話へと走った」に続く文を選ぶ。第2段落で，おばあさんの誕生日パーティーをしたいというジェニーの提案を受け，父親はいいレストランがあるので予約してあげると言っているので，**エ**の「なぜなら彼は娘を手助けしたかったから」が適切。

（要約）
ジェニーは祖母が好きで，祖母の誕生日パーティーをしたい，と父に言った。父は，賛成してくれ，レストランを予約してあげよう，と言った。

5 「王は若者たちが持ってきた植物を見てとても喜んだ」に続く文を選ぶ。第6段落第3文や第7段落最後の文から，**ア**「なぜならそれらの植物は役に立ち，彼はだれが新しい王に最適かわかったから」が適切。

（要約）
次の王として国をよりよくしてくれる最適な人物を見つけたかった年老いた王は，宮殿に国の若者たちを全員呼び，彼らから王を選ぶと宣言した。王は彼らに種を渡し，それを育てて半年後に持ってくるよう指示した。その植物を見て次の王を選ぶというのだ。半年後，ジョーだけが植物の育っていない鉢植えを王に見せた。王は「種はゆでられたものだった」という真実を明かし，ジョーが次の王に最適だとわかった。

 長文読解（絵や数字を読みとる）

本冊
P.43

解答

1 ア **2** イ
3 A twenty-five
　　B first

解説

1 高也が，下線部のあとに続く3つの発言でグラ

フの説明をしている。「グラフは生徒が家事を
する頻度を表している」→「最も多数の生徒が
毎日家事をしている。最も少数の生徒が家事を
まったくしない」→「週に1，2回家事をする生
徒より，週に4回家事をする生徒のほうが数が
少ない」に合うのは**ア**。

（要約）
　高也は，以前は母親に弁当を作ってもらってい
たが，今は自分で作るようになったと，アンに
話す。ハマ先生が見せた，生徒たちが家事をす
る頻度を示したグラフ，そして「私たちは家族
の一員なのだから，家事をするべきです」とい
う先生の言葉が高也を変えたのだ。

2 「例えば，□□の森林率を見てください。それ
は50％以上だろうと思っていましたが，□□の
森林率は日本の森林率の約半分です」という文。
グラフを見ると，日本の森林率は68.5％で，
その約半分の国は34.1％のCanada。

（要約）
　高志は，地球温暖化について勉強してから環境
に関心がある。環境について調べ，日本は他の
国と比べて森林率が高いこと，国内では岐阜県
の森林率が高いことを知り，将来，岐阜県の森
林を保護するために何か環境に役立つことがで
きたらいいなと思っている。

3 「マークは□**A**□歳のときに，日本での滞在後
□**B**□回目に，ケンから手紙をもらった」とい
う文。第2段落第3文に「私は15歳のときに日
本に1か月滞在した」，第5文に「私はそのとき
から10年間，彼（＝ケン）から便りをもらって
いない」とあるので，**A**には手紙が来た時点の
年齢の25を，**B**には「初めて」となるよう，
firstを入れる。for the first time「初めて」。

（要約）
　自動車整備士のマークは仕事が楽しくなかっ
た。ある日，10年前に日本に滞在したときの
友人のケンから手紙が来た。その手紙には，10
年前に自分あてに書いた手紙が同封されてい
た。

 ## 長文読解
（文や語の並べ替え・補充）

解答　　　　　　　　　　　　　　　本冊
　　　　　　　　　　　　　　　　　　P. 47

1 c　**2** find　**3** イ

解説

1 挿入する文は「いろいろな場所から来た人々も
彼とボランティア活動をし始めた」という意味。
a, bは，まだ会社内での出来事を述べた部分な
ので不適切。dは招待された中学校について述
べた部分。cのある段落は，社長がボランティ
アで会社の近くの公共トイレを掃除し始め，近
所の人たちも加わったことが書かれており，直
前に「彼のボランティア活動は彼をとても有名
にした」とあるので，ここに入れるのが適切。

（要約）
　ある会社の社長が「きれいな職場は社員を幸せ
にする」と考え，自分の会社のトイレの掃除を
始めた。最初は社長1人で掃除を続けたが，最
終的には全社員がトイレ掃除をするようになっ
た。次に，その社長はボランティア活動として
会社近くの公共トイレの掃除を始め，近所の人
たちも手伝った。また社長と彼のボランティア
グループの人たちは，ある中学校に招待され
た。トイレ掃除をするだけで人が変われるのは
「きれいな場所にいると幸せを感じるし，一緒
に活動することが大切だとわかるので親切にな
れるからだ」と社長は言う。

2 下線部は「おお，そうでしたか」の意味で，直
前の文I found my muffler!に対するあいづ
ちの表現。直前の文をヒントにすれば，省略語
を見つけるのは比較的やさしい。did you?が
前の文を2語の疑問形にした表現であることに
注意する。
　設問の英文は，一般動詞過去の疑問文となり，
did youのあとに〈動詞の原形～〉が省略され
ている。ここではfoundを原形findにして入
れる。答えは必ず省略部分にあてはめて正しい
か確認しよう。

（要約）
　ジャスミンがうれしそうに見えたので，ハラ先

生が理由を尋ねたところ，昨日なくした大切な
マフラーを見つけたのだと答える。それは駅の
近くのポストの上に置かれており，だれかが
拾って置いてくれたのではないかとジャスミン
は考える。ささやかな行為の中にも，その人の
親切な心を示すことがあるという話になる。

3 「人々はそのような強いトンネルを持ってうれ
しかった」という文。前文でトンネルの強さに
ついて述べているイが適切。

（要約）

19世紀のロンドン。貨物を輸送する船が川に
かかる橋の下を通過する際，帆が橋にぶつかっ
てしまうという問題があった。これを解決する
ため，川の下にトンネルを掘る計画が立てられ
た。この工事の際，「フナクイムシ」という生
物の持つ特徴をヒントにした「シールド工法」
が用いられ，頑丈なトンネルをつくることに成
功した。小さなものを注意深く見ることで，よ
りよいものを作り出すことができるかもしれな
い。

長文読解
（英文の質問に英語で答える）

解答

本 冊
P. 51

1 ウ
2 (1)（例）(The) university students did.
　(2)（例）It is to plan events for his town
　　in the future.
3（例）(She said good-bye to him) in front
　of the lilies by his house.
4（例）Because he is always kind to them.
　　　　　　　　　　　　　　　　(7語)
5（例1）He was glad (to hear that).
　（例2）He felt glad and he wanted her to
　　read his other poems.
6（例）He started to use English more.
7 (1)（例）To paint mountains and a
　　beautiful river.
　(2)（例）He promised that he would
　　never give up his dream.
8（例）She plays *shogi* on the Internet.

9 (1)（例）(Because she found that) They
　　had the same towel.
　(2)（例）(She joined it for) Three (days).

解説

1 質問は「フランクとロジャーが抱えている1つ
の問題は何ですか」。コンサートのチケットは
4枚あり，フランクとロジャー以外に，そのコ
ンサートは親が同伴しなければならないので，
残るチケットは1枚となる。誘いたい友達は2
人一緒でないと誘えないので，彼らの抱える問
題とは**ウ**の「彼らには2人の友達を誘うのに十
分なチケットがない」が適切。

（要約）

フランクは父親がコンサートのチケットを4枚
入手したので，ロジャーを誘う。そのコンサー
トは親同伴なので，残るチケットは1枚となり，
フランクとロジャーは，ティムとクリス，デイ
ビッドとダニエルは2人一緒でないと誘えない
ので悩む。それでベティを誘うことにした。

2 (1)「だれがこのイベントを計画しましたか」と
いう質問。第1段落第2文に It was planned
by university students for junior high
school students.「それ（＝3日間のイベン
ト）は，中学生のために大学生によって計画さ
れた」とある。Who が主語の疑問文に答える
ので，〈主語＋did.〉の形で答える。

(2)「アキラの夢は何ですか」という質問。最後
の2文に I want to plan events for my
town in the future. That's my dream.「将
来，自分の町のためにイベントを計画したい。
それがぼくの夢だ」とある。my town は his
town とする。

（要約）

中学生のアキラは，大学生が計画した，町の3
日間のイベントに参加した。町の人々も協力し
てくれたそのイベントは，新しい友達を作った
り，年配の人から多くのことを学んだりする機
会を与えてくれた。アキラは将来，自分の町の
ためにイベントを計画したいという夢をもつ。

3 設問のsay good-byeを手がかりにすれば，答えとなる文が見つけやすい。質問は「ジェーンはどこでショウタにさようならを言ったか」という意味。最後から5文目にWe said good-bye in front of the lilies by his house.とあるので，この部分を答える。

（要約）

　ジェーンが父と散歩の途中に，幼いころに引っ越していったショウタの話をした。急にショウタのことを思い出したのは，ショウタと別れるときにゆりの香りがしており，散歩の途中にもゆりの香りがしたからだ。

4 「なぜノジマ先生は彼の病院に来る人々に好かれているか」という質問。第2段落第5文後半にso he〔＝Mr. Nojima〕is liked by them〔＝people who come to his hospital〕「だから彼は彼らに好かれている」とあるので，この前のHe is always kind to〜が答えとなる。設問のis Mr. Nojima liked byを手がかりにすれば，答えとなる文が見つけやすくなる。Why〜?にBecause….で答える答え方を確認しておこう。

（要約）

　私の夢について話します。私が病気のときにいつも行く病院のノジマ先生は親切でいろいろなことを教えてくれます。彼はみんなに好かれています。彼が患者にする3つのことの1つは，趣味について尋ねることです。私も尋ねられて，読書だと言いました。先生は後日，私が教えた好きな作家の本を読んでいて，よいコミュニケーションをとることが患者をみるときの第一歩だと言いました。

5 疑問詞のある疑問文に英文で答える問題。単なる時や場所などを問う疑問文ではなく，How〜?「どのように〜か」と問う疑問文なので，質問の文と共通する語句を手がかりに，様子や状態などを説明している文をさがそう。
　質問は「ケビンはエレンの言葉を聞いたときどのように感じたか」という意味。エレン（she＝Ellen）の言葉は第6文で終わっているので，このあとの文に注目する。第7文前半にI was

glad to hear that「私（＝ケビン）はそれ（＝エレンの言葉）を聞いてうれしかった」とあるので，この部分を答える。

（要約）

　私の新しいクラスの生徒の一人が初めて話しかけてきて「あなたの詩は，私の気持ちを完ぺきに表しています」と言った。私はうれしくて「他の詩も読みますか」と言い，それ以来，私たちはよい友達だ。

6 「高夫は父親と話したあと，英語の授業で何をするようになりましたか」という問い。最後から2文目にHe began to study harder at home and use English more during English lessons.「彼は，家ではより熱心に勉強し，英語の授業中は英語をもっと使うようになった」とあるので，この部分を答える。

（要約）

　国境なき医師団の話に感動した高夫は，医師団に入るためには何をしたらよいかを父親に尋ねた。父親は，一生懸命勉強して医科大学に進学する必要があると言い，さらに，さまざまな国の人とコミュニケーションをとる方法を学ぶことも大切だと教えてくれた。高夫は今，医学生になったら外国へ行って，他の国の学生たちと勉強したいと思っている。

7 (1)「ノブユキはなぜ祖父を訪ねましたか」という質問。第6段落第2文のto paint以下が訪問の目的なので，その部分をそのまま答えればよい。長い文章を読むときは，場面ごとの「登場人物，場所，時」をおさえること。段落が変わると場所や時が変わって，そこから新しい展開をみせることが多い。前の段落との関係に注意しながら起承転結をおさえれば，質問に対する答えがある段落をすぐに見つけることができる。

(2)「ノブユキは父親と将来について話したとき，何を約束しましたか」という質問。第8段落の最後にNobuyuki was very glad and promised that he would never do so.「ノブユキはとても喜んで，決してそうしないと約束した」とある。この発言は，その直前の父親

の発言 "If you promise that you will <u>never</u> <u>give up your dream</u>, I can ...." を受けているので，「彼は，夢を決してあきらめないことを約束した」と答える。

（要約）
高校生のノブユキは，プロの画家になるため，芸術大学への進学を希望しているが，父親に強く反対される。ある日ノブユキは，父親が昔絵画に興味があったこと，ノブユキの絵を大切にしていることを祖父から聞かされる。父親がいかに自分のことを考えているか知ったノブユキは，あらためて自分の決意を父親に伝える。するとようやく，夢を決してあきらめないという条件で芸術大学へ行くチャンスをくれたのである。

8 「ルーシーは将棋が上手になるために何をしていますか」という質問。現在形での質問なので，オーストラリアに帰ったあと，現在のルーシーがしていることを答える。第2段落の第2文参照。

（要約）
オーストラリアからの留学生のルーシーは将棋に興味を持ち，学校の将棋部でルールを学んだ。帰国後も，インターネットで将棋を続けている。

9 **(1)** 「なぜ早紀のタオルは恵子と話す機会を早紀にくれたのですか」という質問。第2段落の第1〜2文参照。恵子が早紀と同じタオルを持っていたのがきっかけで，2人は話すようになった。

(2) 「恵子は何日間バレーボール部の練習に参加しましたか」という質問。第3段落に，早紀に誘われた日に練習に参加し，その週さらに2日間参加したとある。しかし第4段落でそれ以降の練習に参加していないことがわかる。よって「3日間」と答える内容の英文にする。

（要約）
早紀は転校生の恵子を自分が所属するバレーボール部に誘う。恵子は何日か練習に参加したが，その後は来なくなってしまった。実は恵子

はブラスバンド部に入りたかったが，自信がなく言い出せないでいたのだ。それを知った早紀は恵子をはげまし，応援する。現在，恵子と早紀はそれぞれバレーボール部とブラスバンド部に所属しており，親友である。

 長文読解
（下線部の内容を答える）

解答

本冊
P.59

1 （例）アイザック・スターンが演奏したバイオリンの曲を聴いて，感動した人たちを見たから。

2 （例）ヒロシが「日本で英語の教師になりたい」と言ったとき，サラが「あなたならできる」と言って励ましてくれたこと。
(53字)

3 **(1)** （例）自分自身も歩道に自転車をとめてしまったから。

(2) （例）他人にやさしくすれば，その人たちも自分も幸せになれること。

4 （例）プレゼントをもらったとき，その人たちがどう感じるかということ。

5 （例）朝早い電車で勉強している高校生たちもいること。

解説

1 下線部を含む文は「私は彼らを見たとき，<u>バイオリンの曲は多くの人たちをとても幸せにできると本当に思った</u>」という意味。直前の文に「〜多くの人たちもそれ（＝アイザック・スターンが演奏したバイオリンの曲）にとても感動した」とあるので，朝子はそのような人々を見て下線部のように思ったのである。

（要約）
3歳でバイオリンを始めた朝子の最初の夢は，父のいるアマチュアのオーケストラで父と一緒に演奏することだった。9歳になったとき，朝子はプロのバイオリニストになるという次の夢をもつようになった。朝子の最初の夢は今年実現するが，次の夢を実現するために努力をすることが大切だと考えている。

2 解答を，45字以上55字以内で書くという制限の中で，うまくまとめるのが難しかったかもしれない。解答を作成する上で，必要なことをもらさず，かつ簡潔にまとめよう。

直前のyou said to me, "..."と，直後のYour wordsに注目すると，サラが言ったことが，答えに必要な部分となることがわかる。

（要約）

ジュディは母親のサラに古い写真を見せて，写っている男子がだれなのか尋ねた。サラは，高校時代に交換留学生として日本からやってきたヒロシだと言った。サラがずっと持っていたヒロシからの手紙の1通には，当時の思い出がつづられ，ヒロシが「英語の教師になるのが夢だ」と言ったとき，サラが「あなたならできる」と言ってくれたことが励みになった，と書かれていた。

3 (1)下線部は「ぼくはよい生徒ではない」という意味で，第3段落第4文後半のI'm not a good boyと同じ内容。その理由は2文あとにI also put my bike there.「ぼくもそこ（＝歩道）に自転車をおいた」とある。

(2)下線部は「彼の先生の言葉」という意味。ここは健太が人にやさしくして自分もうれしくなった場面なので，第3段落最後から2文目の先生の言葉であるif you are kind to others, they'll be happy and you'll be happy tooの内容を日本語にして答える。

（要約）

ある土曜日，健太はベビーカーを押していた女の人が歩道に自転車がたくさんあって動けないのを助けてあげた。その女性は彼の学校にお礼の手紙を出した。先生は「そのよい生徒を誇りに思う」と言う。放課後，健太は先生に名乗り出たが，自分も歩道に自転車をとめたのでよい生徒ではないと言うと，先生は困っている人を助けた健太をほめ，人に親切にすることの大切さを教えてくれた。

4 下線部の指す内容は前の部分に同じ意味を表す語句がないので，直後の文だと想像できるが，one thingがhowで始まる間接疑問を指すことや，間接疑問の意味がつかみづらかったかもしれない。

下線部を含む文は「私はプレゼントを贈るときに，いつも1つのことについて考える」という意味。直後の文でone thingの内容がhow other people will feel when they get a presentと言いかえられているので，これを日本語にして「～こと」とまとめる。答えがわかったら，下線部にあてはめてみて，適切かどうか確認しよう。

（要約）

里香がカトウ先生の結婚祝いに時計をプレゼントすることをリー先生に話すと，リー先生は中国では時計を贈るのはよくない，という話をした。「時計を贈る」という言葉と「病気の人を最期まで世話する」という言葉の音が同じだからであった。また，リー先生は，「傘」と「別れること」も同じ音なのでカップルには贈らない，とも言い，プレゼントを贈るときには相手がどう感じるかいつも考えると言った。

5 下線部は「父の言葉〔父が言ったこと〕は本当だった」という意味。ヒロシがこのように思ったのは，下線部直前の文I often see ....から，朝早い電車で勉強している高校生をよく見かけるから。具体的な「父の言葉」は，第3段落の最後から2文目にI often see some high school students who are studying on the early morning train.とある。この内容を日本語にして答える。

（要約）

ぼくは高校に入学したばかりのころ，将来ワールドカップでプレーしたいので毎日サッカーに励んでいた。また，外国でサッカーをするために英語も一生懸命勉強したかったのだが，練習に疲れて早く寝てしまうことが多かった。ある日，マークという生徒が文化交流プログラムでシンガポールからきた。スポーツと勉強の両立について尋ねると，「自分は授業中に集中し，わからないことがあると先生に聞くようにしている」と話してくれた。彼と英語でメールを交

換することになり，ぼくは前より英語を勉強するようになった。父にも相談してみた。父も仕事で英語を使うので，毎日早起きして勉強しているのだそうだ。「電車の中で勉強している学生もいるぞ」とアドバイスをくれた。翌日からぼくは，父をまねて早起きした。家を早く出て電車の中で教科書を読むようにしている。

長文読解
（指示語の内容を答える）

本冊
P.65

1 these flowers

2 （例）列車内で飲食すること。

3 （例）飼い主が帰宅し，イヌに会えてうれしいとき，イヌもうれしくて，尾を振ること。／飼い主が泣いていると，ネコが寄ってきて元気づけようとすること。／飼い主が悲しいとき，イヌも同じように悲しそうに見えること。（順不同）

4 （例）忙しくて自分の息子の野球の試合を一度も見に行けなかったこと。（30字）

5 （例）わさびには殺菌作用があるので，昔は薬草の一種として使われていたということ。

解説

1 theyは前に出た複数の人やものを指す。マイクは1枚目の写真を見ながら「タツヤ，これらの花はとてもきれいに見える。それらは何？」と尋ねているので，they「それら」はthese flowersを指す。

（要約）

タツヤはイングランドを訪れ，デイビス一家の家に滞在した。彼は日本から持参した桜の花の写真や日本庭園の写真を見せた。デイビスさんが「次の週末にケントの歴史的建造物を見に行こう」と言った。その夜は皆でタツヤの写真を見て楽しんだ。

2 直前の文を見てdo soが指す内容をつかむ。do soは前に出た〈動詞＋語（句）〉を指すので，それに注目しよう。

do soは「そうする」の意味。直前の文に「列車内では飲食できない」とあるので，if you do so「もしそうすれば」とは，「もし列車内で飲食すれば」ということになる。

（要約）

真二は女性に「列車の中で飲食をすると，罰金を払わなければなりませんよ」と注意された。真二は「知らなかった」と言い，その女性に「ほかにどんな規則がありますか」と尋ねた。女性は，「花をつんだり公園で鳥にえさをやると，罰金を払わなければなりません」と教えてくれた。真二は「厳しいですね」と言ったが，シンガポールの人たちが国を美しくして外国の人に来てもらおうとしていることを理解した。

3 下線部のある文は「これらは動物が人間と感情を共有するということを示すいくつかの例である」という意味。同じ段落の最初For example「例えば」のあとに3つの例が挙げられているので，この部分の内容を日本語にして答える。

（要約）

同じ考えの人もいれば，違った考えの人もいる。違った考えの人と友達になるのは難しいことだろうか。この疑問に動物が答えてくれるかもしれない。「動物はときに人間のようだ」と言う人もいれば，「動物は悲しみを感じるし，ほかの動物を愛することもできる」と言う人もいる。例えば，飼い主が帰宅し，イヌに会えてうれしいとき，イヌも喜んで尾を振る。飼い主が泣いていると，ネコが寄ってきて元気づけようとする。飼い主が悲しいとき，イヌも悲しそうに見える。これらは，動物が人間と感情を共有するということを示す例である。

4 「私はそれをとても申し訳なく思いました」の「それ」にあたる部分を見つける。thatは前文の内容を指すことが多い。英文をさかのぼりながら，「〜こと」の形でまとめる。

（要約）

中学生の晴樹は父親から，中学最後のサッカーの試合に仕事で来られないと言われ落ち込む。

晴樹を気にかけた地域の見守りボランティアの山本さんは，自分の経験を晴樹に話す。山本さん自身も20年前，仕事で忙しく息子の試合を一度も見に行けなかったのだ。しかし地域の人々が息子を見守ってくれたおかげで，息子はさびしい思いをしなかった，だから地域の人々に感謝している，と。それを聞いた晴樹は，自分の父親の気持ちを理解し，山本さんの話を手紙に書いて父親に伝えることにした。

5「これについて知らない日本人がいるかもしれない」の「これ」とは，直前の文にA long time ago, *wasabi* was used as 〜．「わさびには殺菌作用があるので，昔は薬草の一種として使われていた」とあり，この文を指す。文末を「〜こと」にして答える。

（要約）
わさびを知らなかったメアリーに，修はわさびのことをいろいろ教えてあげる。わさびは日本人にとても人気があり，それぞれ好みによって，ほかの食べ物と一緒に食べられている。また，修は父親から聞いた話として，わさびの殺菌作用についても話す。メアリーはわさびのことをアメリカの友達に手紙で書くことにした。

 長文読解
（本文の内容について日本語で答える）

本冊
P. 71

解答

1（例）あなたは，私たちの町のために役に立つことをしてきました。私はあなたのようになりたいです。

2（例）互いに理解し合い，考えを共有しようとすべきである。

3（例）ボランティアとして環境のために何かをすることと，環境についてもっと学ぶこと。

解説

1 本文全体から該当箇所をさがすときは，設問文にあるキーワードを手がかりにすると，さがしやすい。
「驚く」（be surprised）の表現に注目する。

第5段落冒頭にAfter listening to his words, she was surprised and said, "…"「彼（＝山本さん）の言葉を聞いたあとで，彼女（＝裕子）は驚いて『…』と言った」とあるので，"…"の部分を日本語にする。
該当箇所の英文のYou've doneやbe like youを正しく訳せるように注意すること。

（要約）
裕子は高校生で，福岡の太鼓チームの一員である。3年前に奈良と京都を旅したときに太鼓チームに出会い，古い日本の音楽に興味を持った。それで地元の太鼓チームを見つけた。最年長の山本さんに，なぜ長い間太鼓をたたいているのか尋ねたところ，伝統を守りたいのだと言った。山本さんのようになりたいと思った裕子はその太鼓チームの一員になりたいと思った。

2 最後から2文目のTo have good relationships with themのあとに「どうすべきか」という結論が述べられているので，この部分を日本語にすればよい。

（要約）
異種の動物でもよい関係になる例がある。ある動物園のクマのおりに，どこから来たのか，ネコが入っていった。ネコはクマを怖がらなかったし，クマもネコを襲わなかった。互いに同じものを食べ，仲よくなった。人々はこれを見て驚いた。動物園の係の人も「2つの異種の動物のこのようなよい関係はふつうない」と言った。クマが古いおりから新しいおりに移ると，ネコもそのおりに入り，クマとネコはまた一緒に楽しく過ごした。異種の動物が共に幸せに暮らすことができるのだ。私は，世界中の多くの人々も，考え方や言語が違っても共に幸せに生きられることを願っている。

3 最後のアヤコとマユミのやりとりを参照。アヤコのI want to do volunteer work when I start high school.という発言に対し，マユミが "When we start high school, let's do something for the environment as volunteers and learn more about it." と言い，アヤコも "Let's do it!" と同意している

ので，マユミの発言内容を日本語にして答える。

（要約）

中学生のマユミとアヤコは，買い物に行ったとき，駅前にあった桜の木がなくなっていることに気づいた。また，学校からの帰り道，大好きな森にあった木が何本か切られているのを発見し，これからもっと木が切られていくように思われてとても悲しかった。そのことをマユミが学校の先生に話すと，先生は環境について考えることの必要性を話してくれた。自分たちにも今できることがあると知った2人は，さっそく自宅と学校にグリーンカーテンを作ることを考え，さらには高校に入ってからも自分たちの環境を守るためのボランティア活動をすることを決めた。

長文読解
（本文の内容と合うものを選ぶ）

本冊
P. 75

解答

1 ア，オ（順不同）　**2** イ
3 ア，オ（順不同）　**4** エ　**5** イ

解説

1 ア「ビルは洋子の家族にあいさつするために彼女の家を訪れた」　ビルの最初の発言第3文と合う。

イ「ビルはこの近くの工場で働く」　ビルの3番目の発言第2文から，この近くの工場で働くのはビルの父親とわかるので，合わない。

ウ「洋子はたいてい家から歩いて学校へ行く」　洋子の5番目の発言にI usually go there（＝to school）by bike.とあるので合わない。

エ「洋子とビルは終日10分ごとにバスに乗ることができる」　洋子の6番目の発言第1文に「午前中はそれ（＝バス）は10分ごとに来る」とあるが，終日とは書かれていないので，合わない。

オ「洋子は来週ビルに会うだろう」　ビルは最

後の発言で洋子にSee you next Monday.と言っているので，合う。

（要約）

ビルは隣の洋子の家に引っ越しのあいさつに行った。ビルは洋子と同じ高校の生徒になることがわかり，自分の出身地や父親の仕事のことを話した。そして通学方法について尋ねた。

2 本文は内容もつかみやすく，選択肢の英文も後半の部分だけが違うので，解きやすい問題のように思われるが，イのget her help with ～「～のことで彼女の助けを得る」が本文にない表現なので，要注意。

選択肢はすべて「トムは～するためにエミリーに電話をかけた」なので，電話をかけた目的を正しく表しているものを選ぶ。本文の第2文に「大きな試合を見られなかった」，最後の文に「それで彼は彼女に電話をかけて，『試合を録画した？』と聞いた」とあるので，イの「トムは昨日の大きな試合のことで，エミリーの助けを得るために彼女に電話をかけた」が適切。このような問題では選択肢と本文の内容を1つ1つ照らし合わせるとよい。

（要約）

トムはサッカーの試合をテレビで見るのが好きだが，昨日大きな試合を見逃した。そこで同じサッカーファンのエミリーに電話して「試合の録画をした？」と尋ねた。

3 ア「香奈と彼女の家族は，昼食のあとビーチを掃除した」　香奈の2番目の発言第2文と合う。

イ「オリビアはまだ友達と一緒にプラスチックごみを集めていない」　オリビアの3番目の発言第1文に合わない。

ウ「香奈はとても長い距離を移動している日本のごみについての記事を読んだ」　読んだ記事の内容が，香奈の4～5番目の発言と合わない。

エ「何人かのハワイの高校生が，漁師の人たちと一緒に海を掃除した」　香奈の6番目の発言に，漁師と一緒に海の清掃に取り組む日本の高校生のことが述べられているが，ハワイの高校

生についての記述はないので，合わない。

オ「香奈とオリビアは，問題について彼らの友達に話すことに決めた」 香奈とオリビアの最後の発言の内容に合う。

（要約）
　香奈とオリビアが，ビーチや海のごみ問題について話している。香奈が読んだある記事には，誤ってプラスチックごみを食べて死んでしまう海の生物について書かれていたことや，漁師とともに海の清掃活動に取り組む日本の高校生のことを，香奈はオリビアに伝えた。2人は，自分たちにもできる取り組みについて友達と話し始めることにした。

4 話の流れを順に追っていけばそれほど難しくはないと思われるが，本文で使われている英文が少し難しい。時を表す語句に注目して，時間の流れをつかみながら読み進めよう。また先に選択肢に目を通しておくと，本文のどの部分に注目すればよいかがわかる。正解の**エ**のthanked the students for taking 〜 が本文の最後から2文目のthanked them for their helpと同じ内容であることに注意する。

ア「ティムは金閣寺に行く前に銀閣寺へ行った」第1段落第3文と第2段落第1文と異なる。

イ「ティムは銀閣寺へ行くバスの中で何人かの生徒に会った」 第2段落第2〜4文と異なる。

ウ「ティムは銀閣寺が銀でおおわれていることがわかって驚いた」 第2段落最後の文と異なる。

エ「ティムは生徒たちに銀閣寺に連れていってくれたことを感謝した」 第2段落最後から2文目と同じ内容。

（要約）
　ティムはオーストラリアからやってきたALTで，友達に金閣寺と銀閣寺を見るように勧められて京都に行き，まず金閣寺の黄金色に驚いた。次に銀閣寺に行こうとして道に迷い，修学旅行中の中学生に案内してもらった。ティムは，銀閣寺が銀色でなかったことに少し驚い

た。

5 **ア**「トムとクミは長い間仲のよい友達だ」トムとクミは互いに自己紹介していて初対面とわかるので合わない。

イ「トムは彼のホームステイ先の家族の家がどこにあるか知らない」 クミの3番目の発言第5文の問い「あなたはどこに住むのか知っていますか」にトムは「いいえ，でもホームステイ先の家族と駅で会うことになっていて家に連れていってもらう」と答えているので，合う。

ウ「トムは家族と毎年夏に平和公園を訪れる」クミの5番目の発言に「私は家族と毎年8月にそれ（＝平和公園）を訪れる」とあるが，トムが訪れるという記述はないので合わない。

エ「トムはクミを長崎の有名な場所に連れていくだろう」 トムの7番目の発言より，トムがクミに長崎の有名な場所に連れていってくれるように頼んでいるので合わない。

（要約）
　クミは電車の中で交換留学生のトムに会い，彼が同じ高校に来ると知って喜ぶ。クミはトムに長崎にはすてきな場所がたくさんあると言い，今度の日曜日に彼を有名な場所に連れていくことになった。

 長文読解（要約文を完成させる）

解 答

本冊
P.81

1 （例）important
2 A more interesting　B tell
3 **(1)** （例）playing
　　(2) （例）difficult
　　(3) （例）learned
　　(4) （例）dream

解 説

1 本文が長いので，該当箇所を見つけるのが難しい。また，要約文が本文と同じ内容を違った言い方にしていることにも注意する必要がある。

まず，要約文の空らんの前後に注目し，どんな品詞が入るか考えよう。〈it is ～ for＋人＋to＋動詞の原形〉「(人)にとって…することは～だ」から形容詞が入ることが予想できる。

空らんを含む文は「だから，よく食べることや運動することと同じように，私たちにとって十分睡眠をとることも（　）だ」という意味。第2段落第1文に「十分睡眠をとることはよく食べることや運動することと同じくらい大切だ」とあるので，important「大切な」を入れる。

【全訳】

今日，私たちの社会での生活は，ますます便利になっている。24時間営業のレストランや店もある。私たちが望めば，一日中インターネットを使ったりメールを送ったりできる。いつでも遊べる，たくさんのおもしろいテレビゲームがある。このような社会の中で私たちの睡眠時間はますます短くなっており，夜遅くまで寝ないたくさんの若者がいる。彼らは多くの時間を使って，テレビゲームをしたり，友達にメールを送ったりしている。しかし，このような生活スタイルがときに私たちに問題を引き起こすかもしれないことを知っているだろうか。

多くの人は，十分な睡眠はよく食べることや運動することと同じくらい大切だと言う。私たちの体と脳は，起きると働き始め，一日働いたあとは疲労する。だから，あらたな一日を迎えるために，夜十分眠ることが必要なのだ。十分に眠らなければ，何が起こるだろうか。

（まとめの訳）

今日のとても便利な社会では，夜遅くまで寝ないたくさんの若者がいて，彼らは短い睡眠しかとらない。この生活スタイルは，私たちにとってよくないかもしれないし，ときに体や脳に問題を引き起こすかもしれない。だから，よく食べることや運動することと同様，十分な睡眠をとることも私たちには<u>大切</u>だ。

2 A「彼（＝ヒロト）は和太鼓を演奏したあとで，自分の国について説明することは，外国の人々とのコミュニケーションを～にすることができると思った」　第4段落最後から2文目に「<u>異なる文化をもつ人々の間のコミュニケーションは，ぼくがもっと日本について説明できたらよりおもしろくなるだろう</u>」とあるので，「よりおもしろく」のmore interestingを入れ，〈S＋make＋O＋C〉の形にする。

B「だから彼は日本についてもっと理解し，その文化について外国の人々に～しようとした」

第4段落最後の文に「日本の文化について学び，それを外国の人に<u>教える</u>ことは大切だ」とあるので，「教える」のtellを入れ，〈try to …〉の形にする。

【全訳】

この前の12月，ケイトはニュージーランドからヒロトの学校にやって来た。彼女はいくつかの授業を受け，1週間ヒロトと彼の同級生と一緒に学んだ。

最初の日の英語の授業で，ケイトは家族，学校，ニュージーランドの生活について話した。ケイトはまた，書道の授業も受け，簡単な漢字を書いた。昼食時，ケイトはヒロトと彼の友達に何枚かの写真を見せた。写真の中でケイトはそれぞれの手に短い棒を持っていた。ヒロトはその写真について彼女に尋ねた。ケイトは「これは，私が学校でスティックダンスを練習していたときに友達が撮った写真です。あす私がそれをする予定なのを知っていますか」と答えた。「はい，先生がそれについて先週言っていました。見てみたいです」とヒロトは言った。

次の日，ケイトはスティックダンスについて説明した。「これはニュージーランドの伝統的な踊りです。難しくありません。一緒に踊りましょう」ヒロトと彼の同級生は，ケイトと一緒に踊りの練習をした。ヒロトはうまく踊れず，ときどき棒を落とした。するとケイトは彼を助けた。ヒロトは外国の伝統を知ることはおもしろいと思った。彼はケイトに「スティックダンスを知ることができてうれしいです。学校でダンスを習うのですか」と言った。「はい」とケイトは答えた。「ニュージーランドではふつう学校でそれを習います。あなた方の書道のようなものだと思いますよ，ヒロト」ヒロトは，どちらの国の生徒も学校で自国の文化の一部を習うのだと気づいた。

最後の日がやってきた。さよならパーティーでヒロトは「ぼくたちはあなたのために和太鼓をたたきます，ケイト。僕たちの伝統的な音楽を楽しんでください」と言った。ケイトは「和太鼓は聴いたことがないです」と言った。ケイトは力強い音を聴いて驚いた。ヒロトと彼の友達が和太鼓の演奏を終えたとき，ヒロトはケイトに「和太鼓を一緒に演奏しよう」と言った。彼女は「一緒におしゃべりをするパーティーを企画していると聞いていたのですよ」と言った。ヒロトは「そうです。しかしダンスのあと計画を変えました。なぜならぼくたちはお返しに文化の一部をあなたに見せたくなったからです。それで和太鼓を演奏することにしました。先月学校祭で演奏したのです」と答えた。ケイトは和太鼓を楽しみ，ヒロトにそれについてたくさんの質問をした。しかしヒロトはうまく答えられなかった。彼は「ニュージーランドについてたくさん知ったけれど，日本のことはうまく説明できなかったな」と思った。それで彼は気づいた。「もし自分が日本のことをもっと説明できれば，違う文化を持つ人たちの間のコミュニケーションはもっとおもしろいだろう。日本の文化について学び，外国の人にそれを教えることは大切だ」

（まとめの訳）

ヒロトはスティックダンスを練習したとき，外国の文化を知ることはおもしろいと思った。彼は和太鼓を演奏したあと，自分の国について説明することは外国から来ている人々とのコミュニケーションを<u>もっとおもしろく</u>することができると思った。それで彼は，日本についてもっと理解し，外国から来ている人々にその文化を

教えようとした。

3 (1)「保育園で働く前は，ユウコは子どもたち
と（　　　）がそこでの唯一の仕事だと思ってい
た」第1段落第6文に「働く前，彼女は保育園
での仕事は小さい子どもたちとただ遊ぶことだ
けでとても簡単だと思っていた」とあるので，
「遊ぶこと」を1語で表す動名詞 playing を入
れ，主語の形にする。

(2)「だが，彼女はアオバ保育園で働き始めた
あとで，先生たちは子どもたちの世話をするた
めにたくさんのことをしなければならないの
で，そこでの仕事はとても（　　　）とわかった」
第7段落第2文前半に The work was very
difficult「その仕事はとても難しかった」とあ
るので，difficult を入れる。

(3)「彼女はそこでの職場体験からたくさんの
ことを（　　　）」第7段落第2文の中ごろに「そ
この先生たちや子どもたちは彼女にたくさんの
ことを教えてくれた」とあるので，彼女の側か
ら見れば「学んだ」learned となる。

(4)「今，彼女の（　　　）は保育園の先生になる
ことだ」第7段落最後の文に「今，彼女は将来
保育園の先生になるために，とても熱心に勉強
している」とあるので，「夢」dream を入れる。

【全訳】

ユウコは中学生だ。この前の夏，彼女のクラスのすべての生徒が5
日間の職場体験をした。彼らは図書館，駅，学校などで働いた。ユ
ウコはアオバ保育園で働いた。彼女は3歳の子どもたちの世話をし
た。働く前，彼女は保育園の仕事は小さな子どもたちと遊ぶだけで，
とても簡単だと思っていた。しかし働き始めたあと，彼女は間違っ
ていることに気づいた。

最初の日，ユウコはクラスの子どもたちと気持ちを伝え合おうとし
た。彼女は，男の子が絵本を読んでいるのを見た。彼女は彼のとこ
ろへ行き，「一緒にその本を読みましょう」と言った。彼は彼女を見
上げたが，何も言わなかった。すぐに彼は視線を落とし，再び本を
読み始めた。それで彼女は「何を読んでいるの。その本はおもしろ
いの」と尋ねた。彼は再び彼女を見上げた。今度は彼女は彼にほほ
えんだ。突然彼は彼女から走って逃げた。彼女はとても驚いた。「私
が何をしたの。彼に何か悪いことをしたのかしら」

昼食の時間だった。クラスの子どもたちは座って昼食を食べ始めた。
彼らが食べ終わったとき，ユウコは部屋を見てとても驚いた。いた
るところに食べ物と牛乳がこぼれていた。子どもたちはうまく食べ
たり飲んだりできないので，そうなったのだ。彼女は部屋を掃除し
なければならなかった。彼女はとても疲れた。

次の日，ユウコが部屋で子どもたちと遊んでいたとき，男の子が女
の子の手から本を取ろうとした。その女の子は男の子を押して，「い

や，やめて！」と言った。男の子は泣き始めた。ユウコは女の子の
ところへかけ寄り，「そんなことをしてはだめ！　とても危ないわ」
と言った。すると女の子も泣き始めた。ユウコはどうしたらいいか
わからなかった。

ユウコが困っていると，保育園の先生たちはいつも彼女を助けてく
れた。ある先生は「小さな子どもたちは，私たちのようにはうまく
他人と気持ちを伝え合うことができないから，先生は彼らを注意深
く見守って，彼らが何を考えているか，何をしたいのかを理解しよ
うとしなければならないのです」と言った。彼女はまた「保育園の仕
事はとても難しいです。でも子どもたちがたくさんのエネルギーを
くれるから，私はこの仕事が大好きです」と言った。

最後の日，ユウコが部屋を掃除しているとき，男の子が彼女のとこ
ろにやって来て「この本を読んで，ユウコ先生」と言った。彼は最初
の日に彼女から走って逃げた男の子だったので，彼女はとてもうれ
しかった。彼女は彼に「もちろんよ！　一緒に読みましょう」と言っ
た。

ユウコは5日間を終えたとき，アオバ保育園で働いたことは彼女に
とって本当によい経験だったと感じた。その仕事はとても難しいけ
れど，そこの先生と子どもたちは彼女にたくさんのことを教えてく
れて，彼らは彼女にたくさんのエネルギーも与えてくれた。今，彼
女は将来保育園の先生になるためにとても一生懸命勉強している。

（まとめの訳）

　保育園で働く前，ユウコは子どもたちと遊ぶこ
とがそこでの唯一の仕事だと思っていた。しか
し，アオバ保育園で働き始めたあと，彼女はそ
こでの仕事は，先生たちが子どもたちを世話す
るのにたくさんのことをしなければならないの
でとても難しいということがわかった。

　彼女はそこでの職場体験からたくさんのことを
学び，今，彼女の夢は保育園の先生になること
だ。

 日本語を英文にする

本冊
P.85

解答

1 (例) ①I have not〔never〕read the book
(before). (6〔7〕語)

②I am going (to go) to the〔a〕library
tomorrow. (7〔9〕語)

/ I will go to the〔a〕library tomorrow. (7
語)

2 (1) (例) I will try (to do) many new
things.

(2) (例) We went to their house by car.

(3) (例) I want you to join our group.

(4) (例) I'm looking forward to seeing
〔meeting〕you.

(5) (例) He told his idea to the old people.

3 **(1)** (例) But there are many things (which 〔that〕) I don't know about water.

(2) (例) I will read books and study about it.

4 (例) What do you like about Japan (6語)

解説

1 ①「～したことがない」は現在完了の否定文で表す。〈have〔has〕never ＋過去分詞〉の形。neverのかわりにnotでもよい。

②「行くつもりだ」はbe going to goかwill goで表せる。また，予定として確実なときは現在進行形でも表せるので，be goingでもよい。主語はⅠなので，be動詞はamにする。

2 **(1)**「～するつもりです」はbe going to ～かwill ～で表す。「たくさんの新しいこと」はmany〔a lot of〕new thingsで表す。

(2)「行きました」はgoの過去形wentで表す。「車で」はby car。「（乗り物）で」は〈by＋乗り物の名前〉で表す。乗り物の名前を表す単語にはa〔an〕やtheなどをつけないことに注意。

(3)「（人）に～してほしい」は〈want＋人＋to ～〉で表す。

(4)「～するのを楽しみにする」はlook forward to ～ingで表す。ここは「楽しみにしています」なので，I'm looking ～.と現在進行形にする。このtoは不定詞をつくるtoではなく，ふつうの前置詞なので，あとに動詞がくる場合は動名詞にすることに注意する。

(5)「（人）に（もの）を話す」は〈tell＋もの＋to＋人〉か〈tell＋人＋もの〉で表す。「もの」に「彼の考え」のhis idea，「人」に「老人たち」the old peopleがくる。

3 **(1)**「～ことがたくさんある」はthere are many〔a lot of〕thingsと表す。「私が水について知らない」を関係代名詞を使って〈which〔that〕＋主語＋動詞～〉と表し，thingsのあとに置く。which〔that〕は省略してもよい。

(2)「～するつもりです」はbe going to ～かwill ～で表す。「本を読んでそのことについて

勉強する」はread booksとstudy about itをandで結んで表す。

4「～のどういうところが好きですか」は「～についての何が好きですか」と考えて，What do you like about ～?で表す。

 長文中の空らんを埋める英作文①

解答

本冊 P.87

1 **ア** (例) Will you tell me about schools in Canada?

イ (例) teachers go to the classrooms.

ウ (例) they start in April.

2 **(1)** (例) my father gave it to me / it is a present from my father

(2) (例) I can do it / it is easy for me

3 (例) know how to make (a) cake / have made one before

解説

1 **ア** 次にOK.と答えたあと，カナダの学校について説明しているので，「カナダの学校について話してくれませんか」と依頼する文を書く。「～してくれませんか」はWill〔Would, Could〕you ～?で表す。

イ「カナダでは先生は全員自分の教室を持っていて，そこで生徒を待ちますが，日本では □□□」という文。「先生が教室に行きます」という文を書いてカナダとの違いを述べる。

students wait for the teachers in the classrooms.「生徒が教室で先生を待ちます」でもよい。

ウ「そこでは学校は9月に始まりますが，ここ日本では □□□」という文。「それらは4月に始まる」という文を書く。「4月に」はin April。

2 **(1)** Aの「それ（＝ギター）をどこで買いましたか」にBが「わかりません，なぜなら～だからです」と言っている場面。becauseのあとに〈主語＋動詞～〉の文の形を続ける。「昨日は私の誕生日でした」，そしてAの「よいお父さんですね」という言葉が続いているので，解答例

のように「父が私にそれをくれました」や「それは父からのプレゼントです」などが適切。
I got it from my father「私は父からそれをもらいました」でもよい。

(2) Aの「このドアを開けようとしているのですができません」にBが「わかりました。私は〜と思います」と言っている場面。I thinkのあとに〈主語＋動詞〜〉の文の形を続ける。解答例のように「私はそれができる」や「それは私には簡単だ」などが適切。I can open it「私はそれを開けられる」やI can help you「私はあなたを手助けできる」などでもよい。

3 「ケーキはどうですか。私は＿＿＿，だからあなたをお手伝いできます」の空らんに適する英語を考える。解答例のように「ケーキの作り方を知っている」や「前にケーキを作ったことがある」などの文が書ける。「〜の作り方」はhow to make 〜で表せる。「〜したことがある」は現在完了〈have〔has〕＋過去分詞〉で表す。
am good at making cakes「ケーキを作るのが得意だ」でもよい。

 長文中の空らんを埋める英作文②

本冊 P. 89

解答

1 **(1)** (例) is carrying〔taking/bringing〕(some) food〔something to eat〕
(2) (例) is bigger〔larger〕than

2 **ア** (例) How long did you stay (there)?
イ (例) What did you do (there)?
ウ (例) Would you like to see it?

解説

1 **(1)**「食料を運んでいる」の部分を書く。「〜している」は現在進行形〈be動詞＋〜ing〉で表す。「運ぶ」はcarry。
(2)「他よりも大きい」の部分を書く。「〜よりも…」は〈比較級＋than 〜〉で表す。「大きい」big〔large〕の比較級はbigger〔larger〕。

2 **ア** ボブが「ぼくは3週間滞在しました」と答えているので，「あなたはどれくらい（の間）滞在

しましたか」と期間を尋ねる文を書く。How long 〜?で表す。How longのあとには〈did＋主語＋動詞の原形？〉の形がくる。
イ ボブが日本でしたことを答えているので「あなたは何をしましたか」と尋ねる文を書く。Whatのあとに〈did＋主語＋動詞の原形？〉の形を続ける。
ウ 「ぼくの家でぼくが撮ったビデオをきみに見せてあげられる」に続くボブの言葉を考える。トムはYes, I'd like to.「はい，そうしたいです」と答えているので，「それを見たいですか」などと尋ねる文を書く。「あなたは〜したいですか」はWould you like to 〜?で表せる。Do you want to 〜?でもよい。

 自由英作文（絵・資料を使った問題）

本冊 P. 91

解答

1 (例) Last Sunday Mitsuo and Kazuo went on a picnic. Mitsuo got up at 6:00 and Kazuo got up at 7:50. Mitsuo ate breakfast but Kazuo didn't eat breakfast. After they walked up the hill for a while, Kazuo stopped. Kazuo was very hungry. Mitsuo was not hungry but they decided to eat lunch by a tree. After lunch they started to walk up the hill again. They got to the top of the hill. (8文)

2 (例) I think computers are important in our life because they are very useful. For example, we can use the Internet to read the news. We can also exchange e-mails with our friends in foreign countries in a day. (3文)

3 (例) Which (movie) do you want to see?
(6〔7〕語)

解説

1 絵からわかることを書き出してみる。
A「ミツオは6時40分ごろ朝食を食べている。カズオは8時ごろ，朝食を食べないで急いで出かける様子」

→B「カズオは朝食を食べてこなかったので，おなかがすいたと言っている」

→C「ミツオとカズオが一緒に昼食を食べている」

→D「ミツオとカズオが丘の頂上に着いて喜んでいる」

get up「起きる」，eat breakfast「朝食を食べる」，walk up the hill「丘を歩いて登る」，get to ～「～に着く」などの表現が使える。動詞を過去形にして書くこと。

2 「私たちの暮らしの中のコンピュータ」というテーマで書く。私たちの暮らしとコンピュータのかかわりについて，資料を参考にして書く。最初にコンピュータについての自分の意見を書き，それからその理由などを書くとよい。具体例を入れて説明すると，わかりやすい文になる。理由は because ～，具体例は for example を使って書く。

3 「"Green World" か "Good Friends" を見ることができる」に続く文を書く。「私は "Good Friends" を見たい」と答えているので「あなたはどちら（の映画）を見たいですか」と尋ねる文を書く。Which (movie) shall we see?「どちら（の映画）を見ましょうか」でもよい。

 自由英作文（手紙文を書く）

解答

本冊
P. 93

1 (bag の例) (Thank you very much for the) bag(.) I've wanted a new bag for a long time. The bag I have now is very old. When I become a high school student, I'll use this bag every day. (30語)

【別解】

(bike の例) (Thank you very much for the) bike(.) I just wanted a new bike. Since my old bike broke down, I've had to go to school by bus. Thanks to my new bike, I don't have to pay the fare.
(32語)

(book の例) (Thank you very much for the) book(.) This is a book I wanted. My hobby is reading books. I am interested in the story of this book. Since I am free this weekend, I'm going to read it. (31語)

(cake の例) (Thank you very much for the) cake(.) Cake is my favorite kind of sweet. Do you like to make sweets yourself? I want you to teach me how to make a cake if you are free before Christmas. (31語)

(CD player の例) (Thank you very much for the) CD player(.) I like listening to music. If I use the player you gave me, I can enjoy listening to my favorite singer's songs. This tool is also useful for me to practice English listening.
(33語)

2 (1) (例) This is my first visit to America.

(2) (例) Shall we eat lunch together?

【別解】Let's eat〔have〕lunch together.／How〔What〕about eating〔having〕lunch together?／Why don't we eat lunch together?

解説

1 5つの中から，自分が書きやすそうなものを選んで書くとよい。30語程度という条件があるので，3，4文で書くことになる。そのプレゼントをずっとほしいと思っていた，だからとてもうれしい，それがあるとどのように役立つかなど，相手に感謝の気持ちが伝わるような文を書くとよい。

2 (1)「これは私のアメリカへの初めての訪問です」と表せばよい。「～への初めての訪問」は my first visit to ～で表す。

(2)「～しませんか」と誘う文は，Shall we ～? や Let's ～. や How〔What〕about ～? や Why don't we ～?などで表す。

自由英作文（自己紹介・説明）

本冊 P. 95

解答

1 (1)（例）My treasure is my dog.（5語）

(2)（例）Because I feel happy when I play with him.（9語）

2 （例）(I want to show her) Karatsu-kunchi (because) it is one of the biggest festivals in Saga(.)

【別解】(I want to show her) Yoshinogari (because) this is a very old Japanese village(.)

3 (1)（例）I visited many places in Kyoto with my friends.（9語）

(2)（例）I thought they were very beautiful.（6語）

4 （例）I like playing baseball because it's very exciting. I started playing baseball when I was ten. I want to be a good baseball player like Ichiro.（3文）

【別解】My hobby is cooking. I cook with my mother every Sunday. I like making sandwiches. My father enjoys eating my sandwiches.（4文）

5 （例）I would like to talk about our school life. School starts in April and finishes in March. We have a summer vacation in July and August. We have five to six classes from Monday to Friday. We enjoy club activities after school.（5文）

解説

1 (1)「私の宝物は〜です」は My treasure is 〜. で表す。(2)で理由が書きやすいものを選んで書くとよい。

(2)理由は Because 〜.「（なぜなら）〜だから」で表す。

2 ロンドンから来る友達に自分の生まれ故郷，または現在住んでいる町の何を見せたいかを表す文を完成させる。□内は，「私は彼女に（　）を見せたい，なぜなら（　）だから」という

内容。理由が書きやすいものや場所を選んで書くとよい。

3 (1)「中学校時代の思い出」というテーマなので，修学旅行，文化祭，体育祭，部活動などの思い出について書くとよい。過去の文で表すこと。

(2)「あなたはどう思いましたか」という問いに答えるので，I thought (that) 〜.「私は〜と思いました」の文で書く。

4 自分の趣味について書く。「私の趣味は〜です」は My hobby is 〜. で表す。hobbyという単語を使わなくても，「私は〜が好きです」と考えて，I like 〜. の文で表してもよい。3文以上書くので，その趣味を始めたきっかけや，いつその趣味を楽しむかなど，自分と趣味とのかかわりを説明する文を書くとよい。

5 設問は「日本を紹介するために英語でスピーチをしてくれませんか」という意味。日本の有名な場所や日本の文化など，何でもよいが，設問を参考に自分が書けそうな題材を選んで書くとよい。5つの英文で書くので，まず日本語で書く内容を簡単にまとめてから英文にしてみよう。